Life in the Kingdom

LIFE
in the
KINGDOM

by Marc L. Kirchoff, D. Min.

Leeway Literary Works

Published by Leeway Artisans, Inc.

Book & Cover Design by Mykle Lee

ISBN: 978-0-9846698-1-3

Copyright © 04/2010 by Marc Kirchoff.

No parts of this book may be reproduced or used in any form or by any means, electronic or mechanical, including photocopying, recording, or by any information storage or retrieval system, without permission from the Publisher.

ALL RIGHTS RESERVED

First Edition

Printed in the United States of America.

Scripture quotations are from The Holy Bible, English Standard Version, copyright © 2001 by Crossway Bibles, a division of Good News Publishers. Used by permission. All rights reserved.

Contents

INTRODUCTION	1

PART ONE -- GOD'S MISSION STATEMENT

MISSION STATEMENTS	7
Concise it is not!	8
GOD'S MISSION	13
What is God's mission statement?	13
God's Mission -- reprise	20
SHALOM	21
The Fall	22
Broken Relationships	23
Pain and Toil	27
Death	28
God's Work to Restore Shalom	29
FROM CAIN AND ABEL TO THE PROMISED LAND	31
JUDGES, KINGS AND PROPHETS	35
JESUS' MISSION	37
Jesus' Mission Statement	37
Jesus' Work	41

PART TWO -- GOD'S VISION

VISION STATEMENTS	45
GOD'S VISION STATEMENT	47
Isaiah	47

Revelation	*50*
Certainty of the Vision	*56*
OUR MISSION	**57**

PART THREE -- GOD'S STRATEGIC PLAN

STRATEGIC PLAN	**65**
THE GOOD NEWS OF THE PARABLES	**69**
Three Parables	*70*
THE GOOD NEWS	**75**
PREPARING FOR THE HARVEST	**79**
PARABLE OF THE TALENTS	**83**

PART FOUR -- GOD'S TACTICS

THE PATTERN	**91**
To explain…	*92*
THE FEEDING OF THE 5,000	**95**
Need	*95*
Resources	*99*
Application	*102*
Results	*104*
THE STORY OF JOSEPH	**105**
Need	*105*
Resources	*107*
Application of Resources	*108*
Results	*118*

JESUS' FIRST MIRACLE — **121**
   Need — *121*
   Resources — *122*
   Application — *123*
   Results — *124*

GIDEON — **125**
   Need — *125*
   Resources — *127*
   Application — *131*
   Results — *133*

THE CREATION OF WOMAN — **135**
   Need — *136*
   Resources — *136*
   Application — *137*
   Results — *138*

ONE FINAL EXAMPLE – THE STORY OF THE BIBLE — **139**
   Need — *140*
   Resources — *140*
   Application — *141*
   Results — *142*

CONCLUSION — **145**

Dedication

To my dear friend and "tech advisor," Larry. You left us too soon – I still need you.

Foreword

First, a disclaimer...

The statements I make herein are based not so much on research as on insight. I did not conduct surveys or talk with focus groups to discover facts, ideas, plans, needs or anything that requires foundational materials.

These are my thoughts resulting from observation of the world, study of the Christian scriptures and experience in life.

They are thoughts specific to life in the Kingdom of God. I do not offer them so much a theological platitudes, but as ideas for your consideration as a co-laborer in the vineyard, to use an overly-worn phrase.

While overly-worn, however, the phrase helps to provide a context for my remarks. As you read, consider my thoughts as one who shares equal status with millions of others. We are, after all, servant-workers in God's Kingdom.

Acknowledgements

A few years ago, as I was studying some of the more familiar scripture passages (ones I had studied many times before!), I discovered the pattern I share in chapter four. I found it in a few, familiar passages, then started seeing it in many other passages, as well.

It is a pattern that repeats over and over and over again. In short passages, in Jesus' parables, in whole books of the Bible. In a variety of settings and contexts, I found this pattern.

So I started writing down the passages wherein I found the pattern. Over the course of several months, I accumulated several stories. I started sharing my discoveries in the form of Bible studies, sermons and Sunday School lessons.

One day, someone suggested I publish my discovery. So I began to clean up my notes, format the lessons and sermons into a readable form. And save them on disc. I thought, at one point, I was ready to move forward. Then, the unthinkable – the flash drive on which my material was stored failed.

I was using it one morning, writing and saving. Then I came back to it later the same afternoon and the computer would not read the disc. I tried it on another computer – nothing. I tried using different programs to open the documents – to no avail.

I took the disc to some of my "tech" friends. Nothing. I tried prayer.

I finally called a dear friend who works in the computer tech department of a large, national corporation.

He made several suggestions. None worked. He even spent some time on the phone walking me through the process of diagnosing problems.

After some time, he asked, "Do you have a window in your office?" Strange thought, but, yes, I did. "Take your flash drive to the window, open the window and throw it out."

"My office is in the basement. If I throw anything out the window, it just sits there in sight."

"Hmmmm...do you have a hammer?" Honestly, I did – and I used it!

All the material was lost! I resigned myself to the fact that, if, indeed, I was to share my findings, I would have to reproduce it all from scratch.

So I enlisted help. At the time of the demise of my flash drive, I was preaching at a church in rural Indiana. Their pastor of some 39 years had died a few months earlier and the congregation needed someone to fill the pulpit on Sunday mornings and evenings, with a commitment to stay until they found a new pastor.

I tried to make Sunday evenings a bit more casual and took a teaching, rather than preaching approach. I also used long series of lessons to keep folks engaged in Bible study.

Then, an idea. I explained my dilemma to the congregation. I described the pattern I had discovered many months earlier and enlisted their help. I asked them to study their Bibles and find stories and passages where the pattern is found and bring their findings to me. I offered a prize for the person who brought in the most material. One man brought in some 27 passages (and won the prize, of course).

My little contest provided abundant fruit. I was able to re-discover many of the passages I had used in my original documents. Moreover, the saints found many other stories and passages that reveal the pattern – some very insightful! In fact, I wound up giving two prizes – one for quantity and one for quality. One middle school student brought one of the most insightful discoveries of the series. I will share it later in chapter four.

Now, a confession. Just about the time I had collected all the material for this book, I began to doubt whether I should or needed to share it with others. On the one hand, I felt I owed it to the good folks at Friendly Grove Baptist Church and my friends who had tried to help restore the information. On the other hand, I felt it a bit arrogant to think I could author anything that would keep others' attention, let alone inspire them.

I also considered that there may be a reason God allowed all that material to be lost. Perhaps it was his way of saying, "it really wasn't worth sharing – you need to focus energy on something else."

Then, on one of my daily walks through our neighborhood – the ones where I talk to God and let him speak to me (I don't do iPods) – he let me know that I really do need to share this with the world (well, at least with more than my normal circle of influence).

I finally decided that the reason I lost the material was not that it was not important. It was not because God did not want me to share it. It was not so much that I needed to change my focus. I believe it was God's way of telling me that I need to take information that I have collected over the course of many years and reformat it, throw some of it out, include new material and put forth my best effort – not just a collection of nice stories from the Bible.

So, here I am again at my computer, sharing my findings, but with new clarity and inspiration. So, without further adieu, I present for your consideration a unique perspective on life in God's Kingdom.

Introduction

OVER THE COURSE OF MY LIFE in the working world, I have been blessed to work in both secular and sacred settings. I use the term "blessed" intentionally. I will admit that there have been seasons when I did not feel particularly blessed, but, in retrospect, I can honestly say that even the more challenging times were very educational.

I could write volumes about the things I have learned, but I want to focus on one specific area. I want to share how, even in the most secular settings, I have seen biblical principles implemented.

In the secular settings, these biblical principles were not always recognized as such. In fact, rarely were they recognized at all. Yet they were implemented – many times as if the person putting things in motion had full cognizance of the source.

On occasion, the implementation of biblical principles made me smile. Mostly because the person implementing them was thoroughly secular – on occasion even atheistic – in his/her management theories. What made me smile even more was when the principles were implemented effectively resulting in success!

Of course, there were times when I really wanted to tell everyone what was done, how it was biblical and, therefore, successful. But, in most cases, I held my tongue.

Now I have the opportunity, in the form of this book, to share my smug self-righteousness. Of course, the purpose of this document is not to gloat (as much as I would like to). Rather, I want to share how the biblical principles are applied successfully in both secular and sacred settings.

I share in the context of a sacred corporation. Now, you say, that sounds like a contradiction in terms. I use the phrase, however, to demonstrate how the sacred and secular can, do, and should intersect.

My thesis here is that biblical principles apply in all of creation. We, as Christians know that fact – at lease we should. But I am not always convinced that church folk believe that the secular should intersect with the sacred.

For example, many say that politics and religion do not mix. Separation of church and state is, ironically, sacred to many a political scientist, and to many in the church. In fact, this separation is a creation of humanity – politicians, in particular.

If one reads the scriptures carefully, however, the mix of politics and religion is obvious. After all, it was Caiaphas, the High Priest who said, "It is better that one man die for the sake of the nation." Caiaphas was the ultimate politician of his day – and the chief religious leader at the same time.

In fact, politics and religion do mix, every day, on Capital Hill, Washington and across the USA and around the world. Our faith intersects with our lives on a daily basis – and it should.

So, I posit, the principles I discuss in the following pages are relevant for every day life in the Kingdom. As people of faith, we are all members of this sacred "corporation." And, as members of the corporation, we are charged with being active, productive members of the team which is responsible for the products created in the corporation.

So, let's look at the principles as if they are foundational to this sacred corporation – because they are!

So, what is life in God's Kingdom all about? In the following pages, we will explore some images that, I hope, give insights into what it means to be an active, productive part of God's plan for creation.

Part One -- God's Mission Statement

LIFE IN THE KINGDOM MEANS being part of a well-run organization. Members of any effective organizations are guided in their work by a mission statement.

When God began his work in creation, he had a plan in mind. He started with a mission.

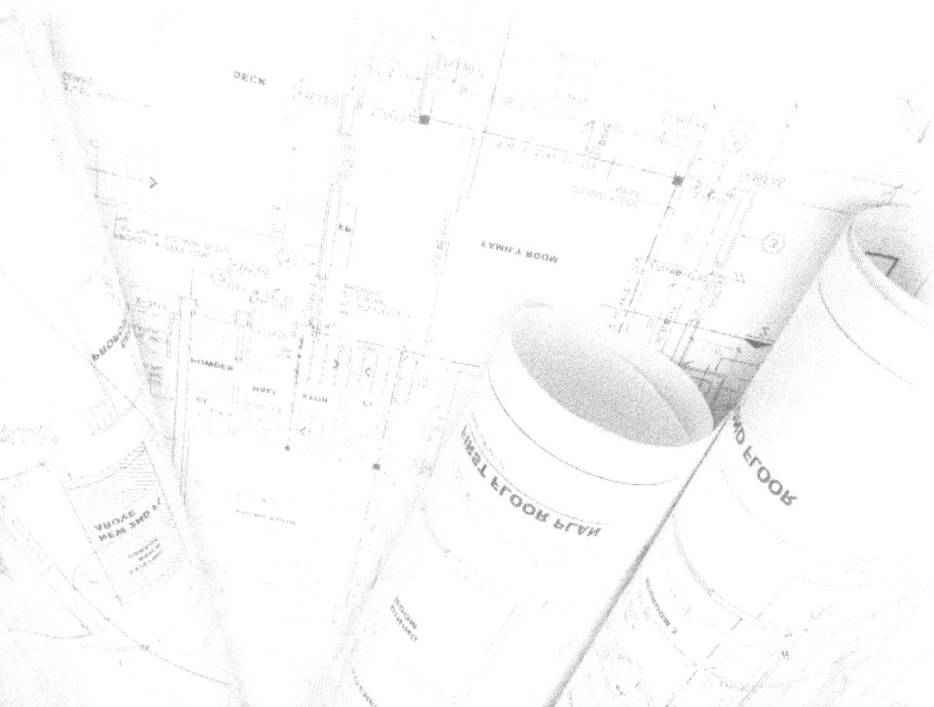

PART ONE — ... A ... STATEMENT

... THE KINGDOM ... a ... ...
organization ... and ... other ... organizations
... guided their work in a different manner.

When God began his work in creation, he had a plan in
mind. He started with a mission.

Mission Statements

MUCH HAS BEEN SAID and written about mission statements. We write mission statements for businesses, non-profits and churches. We even create mission statements for our families and ourselves.

So what is a mission statement? It is a concise statement that describes why we exist, our purpose. It is the boundary that is set for what we do. Let me expand...

If you were to collect mission statements from businesses and organizations around your town, you might be overwhelmed. Not by the volume of statements, however. In fact, I dare say that most businesses in your town probably do not have a written mission statement. Non-profit organizations seem to have a better handle on the concept, so you would have better luck in that arena.

Unfortunately, most mission statements are way too long. People in most organizations will be able to tell you what they do (in fact, what their mission is). But most will likely not be able to produce a a document that states the organization's reason for existence.

Those that do produce a written statement will likely offer a half- to full-page document – maybe even longer! More than likely, that piece of paper is the work of a committee who sought to incorporate every idea that they and all other organization members suggested.

Concise it is not!

I was once chair of a committee assigned the task of writing a mission statement. You've heard of herding cats. This was more like herding ants. Everybody looking very busy. All headed in different directions.

When I tried to steer them in the same direction, one, two or more would change course. Eventually, we all gave in and agreed to a half-page, three-paragraph statement that summarized everything anyone had said over the course of six months worth of meetings. The boss was happy, so we were happy!

To be effective, a mission statement should be brief. No more than a sentence or two. It should incorporate, not every idea offered by every employee, but activity done by every employee that is consistent with the reason for existence.

A good measure of a mission statement is that every employee or member of the organization should be able to recite the mission from memory at a moment's notice.

Longer statements are not memorable. I dare say no one -- not even members of the mission creation committee or the CEO -- will be able to recite a long mission statement from memory. There may be a few who can "kind of describe it" for you. (Those people probably have a better idea for a more concise statement, by the way!)

A good mission statement should be the measure against which all activity within the organization is measured. Any employee or member should be able to understand the mission statement and how his/her activity fits within it.

Let me state it another way. Every person working on behalf of the organization should understand and be able to describe how their personal activity contributes to the fulfillment of the organizational mission statement.

Allow me to illustrate the marks of a good mission statement using a fictional educational institution as an example. Let's say the school offers classes to ages preschool through high school. Just inside the main entrance, you find a framed parchment titled "Our Mission." You read, "The mission of this school is to prepare the youth of our city for productive lives in higher education, industry and community service."

Not a bad statement on the brevity scale. It is fairly memorable. You stop a couple of faculty members and they recite it immediately. The custodian down the hall even has it on the tip of his tongue!

On the counter in the principal's office, however, you find a calendar of activities. On it you see listings for civic meetings, continuing education classes for adults, recreational activities for the elderly and disadvantaged, and even the community picnic! While it could be argued that the civic events provide an opportunity for students to become interested and active in their community, the other activities certainly do nothing to fulfill the stated mission targeting youth.

The board, principal and other leaders need to consider where their true mission lies and reel in some of the extracurricular activities.

As you peek in one of the classrooms, you find a member of the faculty conducting a raffle to raise money for the local Little League. You would certainly question whether that teacher is fulfilling her duties. You might also find her in the unemployment line in a few days, as well!

Granted, this illustration is a bit over the top. Such brash breaches of mission are unlikely in organizations that have a well-written mission statement. Employees understand the mission and conduct their work in such a way so as to fulfill the mission. Administrative staff is in place to evaluate all activity and to ensure compliance.

But, I hope the illustration has helped to solidify in your mind what a good mission statement is, and what it accomplishes for an organization. Understanding these concepts will help in understanding why I believe God's mission statement is what it is. More importantly, knowing the purpose of a good mission statement reveals to us the importance of understanding God's mission statement for

His Kingdom. It is that mission statement that we now set out to discover, understand and, ultimately, fulfill.

God's Mission

Now that we understand what a good mission statement is, let me ask what I believe to be an important question for every member of the Kingdom of God to consider:

What is God's mission statement?

If God has a mission statement (and I, of course, believe that he does) then it guides all of his activity - past, present and future. To discover his mission, then, we can look at what God has been doing. I doubt, after all, that God would do anything counter to his own mission.

Creation

So let's start where God started - "in the beginning." And as we study, let's look at it with new eyes. Let's read what God does and see if there is an underlying theme that gets at what God is up to.

As we consider chapter one of Genesis, we recall all that God created. Heavens and earth, waters and land, plants and animals ... and humanity.

Now, at this juncture, I will confess my first assumption. I have assumed that God had a purpose in mind prior to creation.

We have all heard the expression, "He's on a mission." I remember my parents using this phrase frequently. It describes someone who is adamantly dedicated to accomplish something – usually with extreme (sometimes overzealous) enthusiasm. No one can distract or keep a person "on a mission" from fulfilling whatever it is they have their mind set upon.

I recently crossed paths with my nephew who was selling popcorn to raise funds for his local scout troop. He was "on a mission." He tugged at my arm and asked, "How many boxes of popcorn would you like?" As opposed to, "Would you like to buy some popcorn to support our scout troop?"

After ordering a box, I asked a question about school. But, by the time the words were out of my mouth, my nephew was off to corner another vict...customer. His "mission," I discovered later, was to raise $400 by the end of the next week. He had no time to spare.

I believe God was "on a mission" when he started creation. I do not believe he was just looking for something to do because he was bored. And I do not believe anyone or anything else motivated him to create. After all, "in the beginning," there was only God.

He himself determined to create - with a purpose in mind. And that purpose guided his every action. God had a mission statement prior to creation. And that mission has not changed one iota since that time (but more on that idea later).

Having stated the assumption that God had a purpose, a mission in mind prior to creation, we can now try to discover what it was.

For we know that God accomplished what he set out to do. After all, when he finished, he said that it was "very good." If God was pleased with what he had done, then it must have fulfilled what he had in mind before starting. He accomplished his purpose, his mission.

Order Out of Chaos

> *In the beginning, God created the heavens and the earth. The earth was without form and void, and darkness was over the face of the deep. And the Spirit of God was hovering over the face of the waters.*
>
> **Genesis 1:1-2**

Biblical scholars have wondered and argued whether God created "ex nihilo" (from nothing) or whether he took a preexistent chaos and created order. Not that I can settle the argument (far be it from me to spoil all the fun), but I do have a picture of creation that incorporates both views.

I picture God like a potter (a very biblical illustration, by the way).

At first, the potter's wheel is void/empty ("nihilo"). Then the potter plops a big, ugly, slimy pile of goo onto the wheel. He begins to spin the wheel, leaning forward to shape the chaotic heap of clay. As the potter hovers over the emerging form, an observer begins to see familiar shapes in the clay (order out or chaos). And, of course, eventually, the potter makes something very beautiful, viable and pleasing – very good.

This is the picture I have of God in creation. Creation "ex nihilo" and order out of chaos. And it is the order that God creates that reveals to us his mission in creation.

So let's look at what he did. But let's look deeper than the creatures. Let's look at how the parts made up the whole.

First, note the organization. Light separated from darkness. Light from various sources – some greater and some lesser. Waters were separated. Waters were then separated from the land. Animals were created – some to live in the air, some to live on the land and some in the sea (okay, and some in combination). A place for everything and everything in its place.

See, too that God creates plants. For what purpose? After creating humans, he tells them that he has created the plants and trees for food.

And God said, "Behold, I have given you every plant yielding seed that is on the face of all the earth, and every tree with seed in its fruit. You shall have them for food.

> And to every beast of the earth and to every bird of the heavens and to everything that creeps on the earth, everything that has the breath of life, I have given every green plant for food." And it was so.
>
> **Genesis 1:29-30**

Something is missing here. Did you notice? I find it interesting that there are no carnivores at this point in creation! Both humanity and animals were to eat plants and fruit of the trees. God said nothing about humans eating animals or animals eating other animals. I am not advocating vegetarianism, but we will talk more about this later!

After completing creation, God also established an organizational chart, as it were. He told the man and woman to be fruitful and multiply. He also told them to "fill the earth and subdue it and have dominion over the fish of the sea and over the birds of the heavens and over every living thing that moves on the earth." (Genesis 1:28) Humanity was given stewardship over all that God had created.

In chapter two of Genesis, we read a more detailed account of how God created the animals and woman.

> Then the Lord God said, "It is not good that the man should be alone; I will make him a helper fit for him." Now out of the ground the Lord God had formed every beast of the field and every bird of the heavens and brought them to the man to see what he would call them. And whatever the man called every living creature, that

was its name. The man gave names to all livestock and to the birds of the heavens and to every beast of the field.

Genesis 2:18-20

Note that animals were originally created to serve as helpers. While not one of the animals that God created was the <u>ideal</u> helpmate, I see no word that rescinds this original intent. Therefore, I think it safe to assume that the relationship of humanity to animals in creation was one of master to helper.

This concept in no way allows for animal cruelty. Quite the opposite, in fact. Think about it. If someone or something is brought to you to be your helper, you dare not abuse it. If you do, a person will (or should) leave you to fend for yourself. A tool, once broken, will be of no use. Masters and helpers must be in harmony to work best - to be most effective and efficient – as God designed.

When woman was created, she was so much the fulfillment of what God had in mind for the man, that she became co-equal with the man. "Therefore a man shall leave his father and his mother and hold fast to his wife, and they shall become one flesh." (Genesis 2:24). The woman became the ultimate helpmate and assumed a position with the man as ruler and steward over creation.

It is only after the assignment of stewards that God looks at all that he has done and calls it "very good" (Genesis 1:31). So we must assume that all the good he created prior to the assignment of stewardship only fulfilled his mission in part. It is when he took what he created and organized it and established the relationships that creation was to have in and among each other that God looked upon his purpose as fulfilled.

So we can, I believe, safely assume that God's mission was not just to create, but to create something that continued to live in harmony, in correct relationship as assigned by God. The order that God created, the relationships within that order, when operating according to God's plan, constituted complete fulfillment of his mission.

Some argue that science and religion stand in opposition to one another. I strongly disagree. I believe the two, as part of creation, were given to us as part of the wholeness that God created. God gave us scientific curiosity and ability to help us understand all he created.

Science continues to help us understand how nature works. And each new discovery reveals a bit more of the complexity of the relationships God implanted in and among his creation. And with each new discovery, we see how beautifully whole, correct and appropriate are the relationships God implanted in us and in all creation.

Genesis chapter one and two tell us who created what and why. Science continues to reveal when, where and how he created. Together they build the foundation for God's mission.

God's Mission -- Reprise

So, is there one concise description of everything God accomplished in creation? Is there one guiding statement or principle that God looks to in all of his activity? Is there one overarching principle we, as members of the Kingdom, should be striving to fulfill?

When I challenge a group (a Sunday School class or a Bible Study group) to state God's mission statement, I usually get a pretty quick response - "Love!"

Not a bad answer - certainly part of what God is all about. But I would argue that there is an even greater mission that God has in mind. Something I believe to be a bit more comprehensive.

Pressing further, I usually begin to hear longer, deeper, and more theologically thoughtful answers: salvation, grace, reconciliation. All great answers. And all, I believe, are incorporated in God's mission.

I believe God's mission statement is very concise and memorable. Everyone who is a member of God's Kingdom can memorize and verbalize it at a moment's notice. In fact, I believe it can be stated in one word.

SHALOM

GOD'S MISSION STATEMENT is just this – Shalom. Now, I know the first thing that goes through every mind when they see that word: peace. In fact, the Hebrew word "shalom" is translated "peace" practically universally in the English language.

The idea of peace, the absence of conflict, is certainly incorporated into the Hebrew concept of shalom. But shalom is much greater than peace. In fact, I am sure that we cannot capture the entire essence of shalom in one word.

Shalom, in its ultimate expression, is "a state of wholeness or completeness." True shalom includes wholeness of the physical, mental and spiritual. Such wholeness would, of course, include political peace. By definition, it must also include the completeness of all relationships between and among humans, nature and God.

I admit immediately, that this definition does not adequately describe what true shalom encompasses. But when shalom is disrupted, we begin to see the full implications of what was lost.

The Fall

Notice to this point I have been using past tense. God was pleased with creation. The creatures made up the whole of creation. The reason I have used past tense is that the original purpose, mission of God (shalom) was fulfilled initially in creation. But it was damaged in short time by the creatures.

Now we turn to Genesis chapter three - where shalom is destroyed.

We all know the story of the fall - both the account in Genesis three and from our own, personal experience! What is most important for our present discussion, however, is to look at the consequences of sin that ruined the shalom that God had created.

Having defined shalom as wholeness, we need to consider the brokenness that entered the human experience as the result of sin. Let's take things in order as they happened in the Garden that day.

> Now the serpent was more crafty than any other beast of the field that the Lord God had made. He said to the woman, "Did God actually say, 'You shall not eat of any tree in the garden'?" And the woman said to the serpent, "We may eat of the fruit of the trees in the garden, but God said, 'You shall not eat of the fruit of the tree that is

in the midst of the garden, neither shall you touch it, lest you die.'" But the serpent said to the woman, "You will not surely die. For God knows that when you eat of it your eyes will be opened, and you will be like God, knowing good and evil." So when the woman saw that the tree was good for food, and that it was a delight to the eyes, and that the tree was to be desired to make one wise, she took of its fruit and ate, and she also gave some to her husband who was with her, and he ate. Then the eyes of both were opened, and they knew that they were naked. And they sewed fig leaves together and made themselves loincloths.

Genesis 3:1-7

Broken Relationships

After the man and woman took a bite out of God's plan (pun intended!), note that they hid from God. So, right away, we know that the relationship between God and humanity was, at least, strained. The man and the woman did not want God to see them and they certainly did not want to see God. Broken relationship with God was the first victim of sin.

When God finally found them (it did not take long!), he confronted them. And, when confronted, the man and woman began placing blame.

First, the man blamed the woman for causing him to disobey. "The woman whom you gave to be with me, she gave me fruit of the tree, and I ate." (Genesis 3:12) At least he acknowledged his own decision to eat! The second casualty - broken relationship between human beings.

And note that he also tried to place some blame on God. "The woman <u>whom you gave to be with me</u>...." (Genesis 3:12) Like a child (or anyone of us) – desperate to find a scapegoat! And, in the process, further damaging the relationship they had with God in the Garden.

The woman, too, found a scapegoat (or scape-snake in this case). "The serpent deceived me, and I ate." (Genesis 3:13) The third victim - relationship between humanity and animals.

Now we read that God began the sentencing phase of the trial. First, he cursed the serpent.

> "Because you have done this, cursed are you above all livestock and above all beasts of the field; on your belly you shall go, and dust you shall eat all the days of your life. I will put enmity between you and the woman, and between your offspring and her offspring; he shall bruise your head, and you shall bruise his heel."
>
> ***Genesis 3:14-15***

Then he cursed the woman.

> "I will surely multiply your pain in childbearing; in pain you shall bring forth children. Your desire shall be for your husband, and he shall rule over you."
>
> ***Genesis 3:16***

Then he cursed the man.

> "Because you have listened to the voice of your wife and have eaten of the tree of which I commanded you, 'You shall not eat of it,' cursed is the ground because of you; in pain you shall eat of it all the days of your life; thorns and thistles it shall bring forth for you; and you shall eat the plants of the field. By the sweat of your face you shall eat bread, till you return to the ground, for out of it you were taken; for you are dust, and to dust you shall return."
>
> **Genesis 3:17-19**

But there is a fourth, often overlooked curse. God cursed the ground.

> "...cursed is the ground because of you; in pain you shall eat of it all the days of your life; thorns and thistles it shall bring forth for you; and you shall eat the plants of the field.
>
> **Genesis 3:17**

These consequences and curses point us to some significant, additional detail about the now-tainted shalom that God had created. We dare not skip over these, first, because they represent significant set backs to God's mission statement. Second, as we will see in subsequent chapters, they will be redeemed!

Note how close humanity and God were before sin. In verse eight of chapter three, God was "...walking in the garden in the cool of the day." The relationship to that point was one of friends who walk in the neighborhood after supper.

They walked around the garden together. They talked face to face with each other. I think it safe to assume that they even ate and played together. They may have even put their arms around one another. They could see, hear and touch each other. There was true, direct fellowship between God and humanity prior to the fall.

Today, we think of God as "in heaven" and inaccessible save through prayer. We do not see God, we do not eat with him. We do not walk hand-in-hand with him (not in the physical sense).

Granted, we try to approach the idea of being present with God. We talk of our church building as "God's house." We experience his very real spiritual presence. We talk to him in prayer. But the fellowship and intimacy is nothing like it was in the Garden. It was lost through sin.

The curse on the serpent has some interesting implications, as well. Note the words, "cursed are you above all livestock and above all beasts of the field" in verse 14. I believe this implies that, prior to this, there was a fairly level playing field among the animals.

As noted earlier, there is no allowance for carnivores in the original creation. Animals were given the plants to eat as food. But now, in God's curse, we have an inequality among animals. The serpent is the lowliest. The serpent will now eat dust!

Part of God's curse also separated the serpent and the man and woman. "...I will put enmity between you and the woman..." (Genesis 3:15) And if you ask most men, you will find enmity between serpents and man, as well!

Sometime after the fall, humans began to draw distinction between animals. Remember, animals were originally created as potential helpers for the man. But, after the fall, animals became something quite different.

Some we domesticated. Some of those did become great helpers. I think of the ox, the horse, and, of course, "man's best friend."

Other animals we let go wild. These became our enemy. They run from us now. And sometimes, when provoked or desperate, they attack us and we run from them.

All these distinctions came about not because God told us to, but because the original relationship between humanity and animals had been destroyed.

Pain and Toil

Now, we read what I consider an interesting, but important phrase from God. "I will surely multiply your pain in childbearing...." (Genesis 3: 16 – emphasis added) Note that this is not the entry point of pain in the human experience. Pain was, evidently, part of the original creation - part of God's shalom. More on this in later chapters. For now, just note that the pain was not created, but greatly increased.

In the same light, we see that work became toilsome as a result of the fall. Remember that, in Genesis chapter two, verse 15, God "took the man and put him in the garden of

Eden to work it and keep it." Work, like pain, was part of the original, created order - part of God's shalom. But, in his judgment, God cursed the ground and caused the man's work to become "painful toil" (Genesis 3: 17). As I like to point out, this is the point at which sweat and weeds entered the human experience.

Death

*F*inally, we see the ultimate consequence of sin - death. The serpent argued that the woman would not die when she ate the fruit. In fact, she did not die - at least not on the spot. It was at that point, however, that death entered the human experience. Humanity began the long journey toward death. In a very real sense, man and woman started dying.

God created two very special trees in the Garden of Eden. One was the Tree of Life. One was the Tree of the Knowledge of Good and Evil. It was the latter that was "forbidden fruit" for the man and the woman.

They could have eaten of the Tree of Life any time they wanted (prior to their sin, of course). But, like a child who has been told they can eat anything in the kitchen except the freshly baked cookies cooling on the counter, they went for the cookies rather than the cake!

They could have had life from the tree. They chose, instead, something that looked more desirable, but was, in fact, more deadly.

After pronouncing all the curses, including the death sentence, God made the Tree of Life "off limits." He banished humanity from the Garden. He also set up a sentry of cherubim with a flaming sword to guard the pathway to the Tree of Life. Thus, eternal life was no longer available to humanity as it was in God's original shalom.

God's Work to Restore Shalom

*T*he destruction of God's original shalom does not change his mission statement at all. We see evidence that God has been, and continues to work in and among humanity. I contend that all of God's activity since the fall is aimed at the ultimate fulfillment of shalom - which is still God's mission statement.

This is, of course, consistent with the intent of a mission statement. It is that (in this case) word that directs all activity. It is the guiding principle against which all activity is measured.

Is all the activity of God consistent with the concept of shalom? I think so ...

While I could detail some specific examples from personal history, I will limit current discussion to the broader activity of God. Let's look at how everything God has been doing is aimed at wholeness, completeness - shalom.

From Cain and Abel to the Promised Land

LOOK FIRST AT HUMAN HISTORY following the fall. We see the jealousy of Cain and subsequent murder of his brother Abel, followed by a dramatic downward spiral of the human condition. In Genesis chapter six, God limits human life to 120 years because, "My Spirit will not contend with man forever." Like the parent of those cookie-eating children - "I can only take so much!"

Humanity becomes so bad that God decides to start over. So he sets aside one family of all the earth. The most righteous family he can find. One he believes can carry forth the shalom he intends.

Indeed, he does destroy all of creation, except that which he saved on the ark. Upon their departure from the boat,

God gives the same basic command to "be fruitful and multiply on the earth." (Genesis 8:17)

But very soon after leaving the ark, things began to disintegrate once again. It started with the shame brought about by Noah's youngest son, Ham.

> Noah began to be a man of the soil, and he planted a vineyard. He drank of the wine and became drunk and lay uncovered in his tent. And Ham, the father of Canaan, saw the nakedness of his father and told his two brothers outside. Then Shem and Japheth took a garment, laid it on both their shoulders, and walked backward and covered the nakedness of their father. Their faces were turned backward, and they did not see their father's nakedness. When Noah awoke from his wine and knew what his youngest son had done to him.
>
> **Genesis 9:20-24**

Interesting that immediately following this breach of family dignity, Noah pronounces a curse on Ham. The curse sets Canaan as "... the lowest of slaves... to his brothers." (Genesis 9:25)

Immediately, we have a broken relationship. Brotherly love is set aside and a hierarchy of relationships takes over.

But, not to fear! God is still working toward shalom.

His plan of working with one family thwarted, God next decides to start over with just one man - Abram. He uproots him and sets aside a special place (not far removed from the original Garden, it is believed) to re-establish shalom.

This activity meets with a little more success. We find God at work in providing ancestors as numerous as the stars - beginning with the miracle baby of laughter, Isaac. We read of God's hand at work in saving the people of promise even through the conniving of Jacob and the treachery of Joseph's brothers.

Even when the Hebrews are enslaved by a Pharaoh who does not remember Joseph, God works through the great Moses to free his people and lead them back to the land of promise. Granted, along the way there is a great deal of grumbling and disobedience. But God continues to work - and make progress toward restoring the relationships he originally created.

An interesting study in shalom is the Law that God gave to his people. Most understand that the ten commandments provide the boundaries for all relationships. The first four show how to relate to God. The final six show how to relate to the rest of humanity.

These ten still serve as the standard for God's intended wholeness of relationship. Remember, Jesus came not to destroy the Law, but to fulfill it. If we could ever get it right, we would have complete, whole, peaceful relationships.

But, of course, we cannot. Nor could the Israelites. As they wander, they continue to complain - to the point that God forbids the generation that left Egypt to enter the Promised Land.

Two of the older generation, Joshua and Caleb, are allowed to lead God's people into the land of milk and honey. And there they (well, at least most of them) establish the kingdom on earth that God has in mind (more or less).

In truth, the whole of human history looks like the design of a roller coaster. Many high peaks, and at least as many deep valleys. Lots of mountaintop experiences, lots of sin. But, like a roller coaster, progress is made.

Let's continue our journey to see God's continuing activity toward fulfillment of his mission.

Judges, Kings and Prophets

No period provides a better illustration of the spiral of human history than that of the judges and kings of Israel. The pattern goes something like this. The good times become so good that the Israelites lose their focus on their relationship with God and become distracted by other nations. They begin practicing foreign religions, worshipping other gods and forgetting who got them where they are.

God sends a nation to overtake them as punishment. As the persecution goes on, the Israelites realize and repent from their sin against God and his intents and cry out to him for help. God sends a judge to lead them against their enemy. They are delivered through the power of God and things are great ... for awhile.

The whole cycle repeats many times. You can read it all again in the book of Judges.

Then, the people decide they want a king like the other peoples around them. Here they go again. God tells them how wrong they are to desire a king, but they will not be deterred.

So God gives them what they want (and deserve) - a king. Ironic that, in the reigns of David and Solomon, Israel becomes the kingdom that God intends - at least in terms of wealth and geography. At no other time in history has Israel been so large or so wealthy in comparison to the rest of the world.

But, again, God's people blow it. The kings that follow the "great two" (and even David and Solomon) show their humanity. Their greed for power and lust for what should not be theirs overtakes the righteous intent of their kingdom.

Not even the prophets whom God sends to exhort the Israelites to obedience can bring them out of their plunge into self-destruction. The preaching, the real-life illustrations are ultimately rejected by most. Even when the message gets through and the people repent and are obedient, the good times are short-lived. The nation begins a long, slow spiral toward what ultimately results in the total destruction of Israel.

Fortunately for us all, a faithful remnant remains through a time of exile. And from that "stump of Jesse" comes God's ultimate activity aimed at restoring his intended shalom.

Jesus' Mission

To this point, I hope what has been implicit is that all of God's activity in human history is consistent with his original mission statement. God's work through the patriarchs, judges, kings and prophets was aimed at restoring the wholeness of relationships he created in the beginning.

Let us now consider the ultimate activity of God. But let me be more explicit about how Jesus - God with us - and his mission are fulfillment of shalom.

Jesus' Mission Statement

I believe Jesus was very clear in regard to his own mission statement. It is recorded for us in Luke, chapter 4. It was the day he went to synagogue in his hometown of Nazareth. He was invited to read from God's word. He read from Isaiah:

> *The Spirit of the Lord God is upon me, because the Lord has anointed me to bring good news to the poor; he has sent me to bind up the brokenhearted, to proclaim liberty to the captives, and the opening of the prison to those who are bound; to proclaim the year of the Lord's favor....*
>
> ***Isaiah 61:1-2a and Luke 4:18-19***

To this point, nothing extraordinary had happened. Jesus did just what any Jewish man invited to read would have done - read a passage of scripture.

He continued as any other teacher would have done – with an interpretation of the scripture. After he finished, he sat down and said, "Today this Scripture has been fulfilled in your hearing." (Luke 4:21) Now he had everyone's attention!

In essence, Jesus was saying, "This is what I am here to do and the very fact that I am here is fulfillment of the prophet's words." This, of course, was not well received by the religious leaders. But that discussion is for another time and place.

Jesus was claiming to be the fulfillment of Isaiah (and in our view he was, indeed). It is interesting that he chose to reveal himself at this early stage of ministry, by describing what it is he would be doing - not who he was.

Let's unpack Isaiah's word a bit. Jesus, as fulfillment of Isaiah's words, first claimed to have the Spirit of God upon him. That is, he claimed to be one with God. He in God. God in him. This, alone caused great consternation, no doubt.

At this point, he was not explicitly claiming to be God's son. But it is clear he is claiming special anointing for his ministry. Such a claim would at least merit special examination by the religious leaders - if for no other reason than to protect their own privileged position in society.

So we have one Jesus who claims to be sent with special mandate from God. To do what? Here he was very specific. His activity would involve:

preaching good news to the poor,

proclaiming freedom for the prisoners,

proclaiming recovery of sight for the blind,

releasing the oppressed, and

proclaiming the year of the Lord's favor.

What did this mean to those listening? Most were poor. They welcomed good news. Maybe taxes would be lowered (ha!).

There were many who had been thrown in prison. Some were held lawfully, many just suspects who were threats to the Romans or even to the Jewish establishment. Was Jesus going to lead an insurrection?

As we recall the gospels, we remember many blind people whom Jesus encountered. This was, most likely, a common disability. Great news on the medical front!

Oppressed? The entire nation of Israel was oppressed. The Romans were in control politically. And while they allowed relative freedom of religion, taxation and the laws legislated and enforced by the government were oppressive to the Jews.

The land of Israel had not had what anyone would call a "favorable year of the Lord" in recent history. The pieces were starting to fall into place in the minds of Jesus' listeners.

Already, I suspect, people were starting to whisper the title "Messiah." But Jesus was not addressing political, economic or even medical issues. He was addressing spiritual wholeness.

His claim was to be God's chosen one to bring good news of salvation to the spiritually bankrupt. He would free those in bondage from the downward spiral of sin. He came to shine the light on the truth of God's will to those who were blind to that truth. He had come to release those oppressed by corrupt religious leaders and allow them freedom of true worship to the one and only God. And in doing all this, the Lord's favor would rest once again on the Promised Land.

These words of Isaiah Jesus quoted as his mission statement. And in doing so, he was also saying, "My mission is the same as God's - I come to fulfill shalom."

Jesus' Work

*A*s *you read the gospels, note how every word spoken by* Jesus -- every parable, every sermon - speaks to wholeness. He speaks wholeness of relationship with God and humanity. He uses the restored relationships between shepherd and sheep to illustrate God's intent. He talks about being good stewards of God's blessings.

Every deed illustrates restoration and wholeness. Consider the blind and leprous whom he restored to wholeness of body. Their disabilities sentenced them to separation. Like the rest of humanity, they were imperfect. But because their flaws were outwardly perceptible, the law required that they be separated from the rest of society.

In healing them, Jesus allowed them, according to Jewish law and practice, to join the rest of society in daily activity.

Recall the "unclean" Samaritans, tax collectors and sinners with whom he ate. They, too, were separated from society. The Samaritans by law, the tax collectors by popular (or should we say unpopular) demand.

By eating with them, Jesus declared them "clean" in the eyes of God. He welcomed them into the fellowship of the Kingdom, even if the religious leaders and the rest of society would not.

Consider this, above all: Jesus was truly "God with us." He was walking around, speaking face-to-face, eating with humanity. Just like it was in the Garden of Eden!

All that we read in the Old Testament is consistent with God's mission statement. From Noah, to Abraham, to Moses, to the judges, to the kings, to the prophets, God was working through them trying to restore the original creation - the "very good" that he had established in Eden. The shalom he intended.

God's ultimate activity in his mission was to become one with us. To walk around with humanity again and show us, personally, how he intended things to be. Jesus fulfilled this activity to perfection.

The Jewish leaders had him killed for claiming to be part of God's mission. But God worked even in Jesus' death to eliminate that which was separating us from him - that one hurdle that prevented total wholeness of relationship. In Jesus' death, God punished sin.

That which had separated God from humanity since Genesis chapter three was now eliminated. And the resurrection opened the door for renewed relationship God-to-humanity. Death has been overcome, eternal life is now a possibility again!

Part Two -- God's Vision

EVERY EFFECTIVE ORGANIZATION has a good mission statement. And every good mission statement is accompanied by a good, complimentary vision statement. The Kingdom of God is no exception.

But first, let's define what a vision statement is and what a good one does.

Vision Statements

As the phrase implies, a vision statement describes what things will look like at some time in the future. A good, organizational vision statement describes the state of affairs in the future.

A vision statement complements the mission statement. It creates a tangible image of what the organization will be like when the mission is fulfilled. As such, vision statements usually describe the state of affairs <u>far</u> into the future.

Of course, every organization would like to fulfill the mission, and bring the vision to reality in as short a period as possible. This is usually not the case, however. In fact, most vision statements are never fully fulfilled.

Vision statements are usually idealistic. They paint a picture of the perfectly-operating organization - what happens when everything is working perfectly and all goals have been met.

At the same time, vision statements, like mission statements and all good goals and objectives, must be achievable. If staff and volunteers see that a vision is not achievable, the vision will hold no credibility or authority and will go largely without notice or respect.

For example, let's say our fictional educational institution has a vision that "every adult in the community experiences the benefits of a college degree." Unless the community is exceptional, it is unreasonable that everyone in it will be able to receive a college degree.

There will be some who are mentally challenged. There will be others who see no need and refuse to enroll. There will be some jobs that do not require college-level achievement and college graduates will be passed over.

So, not only is the vision unachievable, it is unnecessary and unreasonable. A better vision would be that "every adult has access to college-level educational opportunities to meet personal needs regardless of economic or personal circumstances." This is achievable (with enough personnel and financial resources). It is reasonable and, in most communities I know of, much needed.

God's Vision Statement

Now let's talk about God's vision statement. Unlike the mission statement - shalom - I believe the vision is stated explicitly. We look to the prophet Isaiah and to John who recorded the vision given to him by God.

And, as we look, let's keep the original creation of shalom in mind. We will make some fascinating comparisons and discoveries!

Isaiah

In Isaiah 2:2-4, the prophet literally sees the vision of God's mission:

> *It shall come to pass in the latter days that the mountain of the house of the Lord shall be established as the highest of the mountains, and shall be lifted up above the hills; and all the nations shall flow to it, and many peoples*

> shall come, and say: "Come, let us go up to the mountain of the Lord, to the house of the God of Jacob, that he may teach us his ways and that we may walk in his paths." For out of Zion shall go the law, and the word of the Lord from Jerusalem. He shall judge between the nations, and shall decide disputes for many peoples; and they shall beat their swords into plowshares, and their spears into pruning hooks; nation shall not lift up sword against nation, neither shall they learn war anymore.

Note the restored relationships seen herein. The Lord's temple will be the chief - no more lusting after foreign gods. Instead, foreigners will be coming to the temple to discover true faith and religious practice - unity of religious belief and practice (and no denominationalism).

Peoples (literally "ethnic groups") will be unified. Peace (as most people think of it) will reign. No more need for swords or other weapons of war. No more armed forces or militia training for war.

More of the vision is revealed in chapter 11 of Isaiah. After describing the one who will reign over the Kingdom in its wholeness, the prophet continues, "The wolf shall dwell with the lamb." (Isaiah 11:6) Everyone knows that the wolf is the natural predator of sheep. And, of course, the baby lambs are the most vulnerable.

But, in God's vision of shalom, we have wolves who do not prey on sheep. In fact, they go beyond ignoring each other. They are living together!

Anyone who has seen one of those "When Animals Attack" videos will be astounded at the next phrases from verses six and seven:

> "...and the leopard shall lie down with the young goat, and the calf and the lion and the fattened calf together; and a little child shall lead them. The cow and the bear shall graze; their young shall lie down together; and the lion shall eat straw like the ox..."

Apparently, in the final fulfillment of God's mission, all relationships between animals will be restored. No more dust for the serpent. No hierarchy in the animal kingdom. The plants will be their source of food. No more carnivores!

And, what's this in verse eight?

> *The nursing child shall play over the hole of the cobra, and the weaned child shall put his hand on the adder's den.*

Not only will the relationships among the animals be restored, but the relationship between humanity and animals will be recreated. This last passage is particularly poignant in light of what we studied in Genesis three. There God cursed the serpent and made him an enemy to the woman.

Here in the vision statement, God, through the prophets, says that the offspring of the woman will play with the cobra and the viper! Children will lead animals that we now considered wild and enemies of humanity.

The picture is one like we saw in Genesis wherein the animals were created to be helpers for humanity.

Cooperation. Restored relationship. Wholeness and completion. Shalom!

Revelation

*T*he last two chapters of John's revelation complete the vision statement for us. And, by the way, is it not interesting that God's vision statement is recorded for us as "visions" revealed by God through two faithful servants. Can God be any more explicit?

We pick up the discussion in chapter 21 of Revelation.

> *Then I saw a new heaven and a new earth, for the first heaven and the first earth had passed away, and the sea was no more. And I saw the holy city, new Jerusalem, coming down out of heaven from God, prepared as a bride adorned for her husband. And I heard a loud voice from the throne saying, "Behold, the dwelling place of God is with man. He will dwell with them, and they will be his people, and God himself will be with them as their God. He will wipe away every tear from their eyes, and death shall be no more, neither shall there be mourning, nor crying, nor pain anymore, for the former things have passed away." And he who was seated on the throne said, "Behold, I am making all things new."*
>
> *Revelation 21:1-5a*

In the fulfilled mission of God, the heavens and the earth as we know them now will be no more. Everything, even that which was "very good" in Genesis chapter one, is gone.

God starts over, once again. Only this time, he does it up even better than before. His vision is for true, ultimate, wholeness, completeness - shalom - beyond anything creation has ever known.

God's vision is for a wholly "new and improved" heaven and earth. What will it look like?

First, no more sea. No need for one. In chapter 22, we read, "...the river of the water of life, bright as crystal, flowing from the throne of God and of the Lamb." (Rev. 22:1) In the beginning, God created a system we all learned in elementary science. Water from the seas evaporates and moves inland in the form of clouds. When the clouds hit the right kind of atmospheric conditions, the water condenses and falls to earth as precipitation. The rain (snow, etc.) provides water the plants need for food and eventually returns to the seas via the streams and rivers.

In the new earth, the water cycle is not needed. All that is required for nourishment and refreshment is flowing directly from the throne of God himself.

This picture is reminiscent of the story of Jesus at the well with the Samaritan woman. After asking for a drink, the woman backs off knowing they are not supposed to interact. But Jesus tells her that, if she knew who he was, she would be the one asking for a drink of the living water that quenches eternally. Seems like a little vision of the future of human relationships, n'est pas?

Back in Revelation, we read that, "the dwelling place of God is with man." (Revelation 21:3) Again, this flashes back to the Garden of Eden on the day of the fall when God is walking around in the Garden during the cool of the day. The fulfilled vision is one where humanity and God walk around and talk and have lunch together.

"...death shall be no more..." (Rev. 21:4a) Introduced in the fall, defeated in Christ's resurrection, death will no longer be part of the human experience in the final shalom.

"...neither shall there be mourning, nor crying, nor pain anymore, for the former things have passed away." (Rev. 21:4b) Remember pain was part of the original creation. It was only increased when God cursed the woman and man after they had sinned. In the final fulfillment of shalom, pain is eliminated entirely.

In verses nine through 21 of Revelation 21, John paints a picture of the New Jerusalem coming to earth.

> *Then came one of the seven angels who had the seven bowls full of the seven last plagues and spoke to me, saying, "Come, I will show you the Bride, the wife of the Lamb." And he carried me away in the Spirit to a great, high mountain, and showed me the holy city Jerusalem coming down out of heaven from God, having the glory of God, its radiance like a most rare jewel, like a jasper, clear as crystal. It had a great, high wall, with twelve gates, and at the gates twelve angels, and on the gates the names of the twelve tribes of the sons of Israel were inscribed -- on the east three gates, on the north three gates, on the south three gates, and on the west three gates. And the wall of the city had twelve foundations,*

and on them were the twelve names of the twelve apostles of the Lamb.

And the one who spoke with me had a measuring rod of gold to measure the city and its gates and walls. The city lies foursquare, its length the same as its width. And he measured the city with his rod, 12,000 stadia. Its length and width and height are equal. He also measured its wall, 144 cubits by human measurement, which is also an angel's measurement. The wall was built of jasper, while the city was pure gold, clear as glass. The foundations of the wall of the city were adorned with every kind of jewel. The first was jasper, the second sapphire, the third agate, the fourth emerald, the fifth onyx, the sixth carnelian, the seventh chrysolite, the eighth beryl, the ninth topaz, the tenth chrysoprase, the eleventh jacinth, the twelfth amethyst. And the twelve gates were twelve pearls, each of the gates made of a single pearl, and the street of the city was pure gold, transparent as glass.

As I read the descriptions of all the precious stones and metals, I notice the absence of something very familiar to us now. In the New Jerusalem, there is no dirt. John is explicit in saying that there is nothing unclean, but I am talking about the kind of dirt in which things grow.

There is no earth - no ground for humanity to work. "Toilsome sweat" and "weeds" have been eliminated. More than that, work itself appears to be a thing of the past! Yea, God!

But what about food? In chapter 22, we read...

> *Then the angel showed me the river of the water of life, bright as crystal, flowing from the throne of God and of the Lamb through the middle of the street of the city; also, on either side of the river, the tree of life with its twelve kinds of fruit, yielding its fruit each month.*
>
> *Revelation 22:1-2a*

The tree of life stands in the middle of the city. It yields twelve crops - one each month - enough for all who live in the city to eat and be satisfied. And with the tree being watered by the river that flows from the throne, there will be no need for the residents to cultivate it.

There are other absences of note. John did not see a temple in his vision. "And I saw no temple in the city, for its temple is the Lord God the Almighty and the Lamb." (Revelation 21:22) The Synagogue, the temple and now the church have traditionally been seen as the dwelling places of God. They are the places where God's people have gone to meet with him.

In the ultimate fulfillment of shalom, however, God, just as in the Garden of Eden, is literally walking around with humanity again. There is no need for a separate place for God to live where his people can come to meet him. He will be ever-present with all his people and the relationship will be ongoing and constant.

John goes on to say, "And the city has no need of sun or moon to shine on it, for the glory of God gives it light, and its lamp is the Lamb." (Revelation 21:23) This recalls the original creation when God created the sun and moon for the expressed purpose of providing light in the day and the night. But in the final fulfillment of God's mission, there is no need for these created lights. The source of all that is needed, including light, is God.

In the new Jerusalem there will be no darkness, no night. Evil (crime) is most likely in the darker times of the day - when there is no light to be shed on what is going on. "...and its gates will never be shut by day—and there will be no night there." (Revelation 21:25) There is nothing evil "going on."

This, too, is in stark contrast to the situation in the garden after the fall. God threw the man and the woman out and set up guards to keep them away from all that God held sacred. In the fulfillment of shalom, however, everything is complete and whole. So there is no need to have gates or guards, or security lights, for "...nothing unclean will ever enter it...." (Revelation 21:27)

I believe the summary phrase for God's vision for the final shalom is found in chapter 22, verse 3: "No longer will there be anything accursed." That which resulted from our sin, that which disrupted the original shalom will be erased by God himself. And in eliminating the curse, God will open the way for wholeness - a complete and perfect state of affairs wherein all relationships between God, humanity and creation will be perfect, just as God had intended in the beginning.

Certainty of the Vision

God reveals his vision in many passages of scripture, both Old and New Testament. We have, no doubt, missed a few in our overview. But know that God reveals his vision very clearly and explicitly to us. And from those pictures, we find comfort and even excitement as we work toward its fulfillment.

In Revelation 22:6, we find the best news of all. "These words are trustworthy and true. And the Lord, the God of the spirits of the prophets, has sent his angel to show his servants what must soon take place." I have studied and taught the Book of Revelation on many occasions. Over the years, I have come to the conclusion that there is but one main message God is trying to get across to us through John.

Very simply stated, Revelation tells us, "We win!" Christians who remain faithful to God and the fulfillment of his mission to the very end - regardless of what it brings - will be victorious with him in the end. And in that, we can be sure.

Unlike many organizational vision statements that go unrealized, God's vision <u>will be fulfilled</u>. It is a great and glorious shalom that awaits us!

Our Mission

SINCE THE RESURRECTION, God continues to work toward fulfillment of shalom. We read about his activity, first in the New Testament church. We read how he visits us now in the form of the Spirit. He walks around with us again!

We read about the early church and its leaders. How the gospel spread, first to the remnant of faithful Israel, then to the Gentiles.

Fortunately for us, God's mission has not ended. We have many great historical accounts of how and what God has been working using his chosen vehicle, the church.

Unfortunately, in that same history, we still see human error and sin. The history of the church is one of great advancements of the gospel to nations who have not heard the good news. It is also a history of human greed for power and righteousness that, ironically, only God can give.

The number of separate church affiliations continues to grow as leaders squabble over doctrinal issues and scriptural interpretations – most of them insignificant hair-splitting. All are counter-productive to what God intends. Shalom - wholeness of all of life, including relationships God-to-humanity and human-to-human and human-to-creation.

But, what is our mission? If we are part of the Kingdom, our mission must be in line with God's mission. That is, we, too, must be working toward fulfillment of shalom. We must be trying to establish what God intends in his vision for the future.

In Paul's letter to the Ephesians, unity is a major theme. Paul writes to the church,

"...making known to us the mystery of his will, according to his purpose, which he set forth in Christ as a plan for the fullness of time, to unite all things in him, things in heaven and things on earth.

Ephesians 1:9,10

In the second chapter of the letter, Paul speaks of the reconciliation of humanity to God.

And you were dead in the trespasses and sins in which you once walked, following the course of this world, following the prince of the power of the air, the spirit that is now at work in the sons of disobedience -- among whom we all once lived in the passions of our flesh, carrying out the desires of the body and the mind, and were by nature children of wrath, like the rest of

> mankind. But God, being rich in mercy, because of the great love with which he loved us, even when we were dead in our trespasses, made us alive together with Christ -- by grace you have been saved -- and raised us up with him and seated us with him in the heavenly places in Christ Jesus, so that in the coming ages he might show the immeasurable riches of his grace in kindness toward us in Christ Jesus. For by grace you have been saved through faith. And this is not your own doing; it is the gift of God, not a result of works, so that no one may boast. For we are his workmanship, created in Christ Jesus for good works, which God prepared beforehand, that we should walk in them.
>
> **Ephesians 2: 1-10**

Paul also speaks of the reconciliation of humanity to one another.

> Therefore remember that at one time you Gentiles in the flesh, called "the uncircumcision" by what is called the circumcision, which is made in the flesh by hands -- remember that you were at that time separated from Christ, alienated from the commonwealth of Israel and strangers to the covenants of promise, having no hope and without God in the world. But now in Christ Jesus you who once were far off have been brought near by the blood of Christ. For he himself is our peace, who has made us both one and has broken down in his flesh the dividing wall of hostility by abolishing the law of commandments expressed in ordinances, that he might create in himself one new man in place of the two, so making peace, and might reconcile us both to God in one

> *body through the cross, thereby killing the hostility. And he came and preached peace to you who were far off and peace to those who were near. For through him we both have access in one Spirit to the Father. So then you are no longer strangers and aliens, but you are fellow citizens with the saints and members of the household of God, built on the foundation of the apostles and prophets, Christ Jesus himself being the cornerstone, in whom the whole structure, being joined together, grows into a holy temple in the Lord. In him you also are being built together into a dwelling place for God by the Spirit.*
>
> ***Ephesians 2:11-22***

Throughout the letter, he writes about the unity of all in one body which is the Church.

In the fourth chapter, Paul exhorts the church to be "eager to maintain the unity of the Spirit in the bond of peace." (Ephesians 4:3) He continues by giving us the familiar statement about the "one-ness" of the body of Christ. He also delineates some of the gifts of the Spirit within that body.

Paul concludes that the purpose of the spiritual gifts is to build up the unified body of Christ, "...until we all attain to the unity of the faith and ... the measure of the stature of the fullness of Christ." (Ephesians 4:13)

Elsewhere (2 Corinthians, specifically), Paul tells us that God, who brought about our reconciliation to him, is "...entrusting to us the message of reconciliation. Therefore, we are ambassadors for Christ, God making his appeal through us." (2 Corinthians 5:19-20)

This is our reason for existence as Christians - members of the Kingdom. Just as Jesus' mission and ministry complemented God's mission and vision, so must ours!

Paraphrasing Paul's words, we are to keep the unity through the bond of peace (shalom). We are to discover, develop and use the gifts God has given to us to work toward the ultimate unity of the faith in Jesus Christ. We are the ambassadors who must take the message of reconciliation to the world. And we must do it "as though God himself were making his appeal through us" (because he is)!

Consider again these words and phrases: one body, unity, reconciliation. All descriptive of the activity we, as members of the Kingdom, must undertake toward fulfillment of the mission and vision God has given.

We all know that we cannot fully bring about what God intends. He has told us that only he can accomplish his purposes. But, in his word, he tells us that we either work with him or we work against him. There is no moderation!

Is everything you do aimed at re-creating shalom? Is every deed creating new or restored relationships with God? With other humans? With creation?

As Christians, we are citizens of the Kingdom on earth. As we see in John's revelation, a new heaven and a new earth are coming. But, if we are to be part of that future Kingdom, we must be preparing for it in the present Kingdom.

In preaching class in seminary, my professor reminded me that every sermon must challenge the listeners to act on what they have heard. While my intent here is not to preach, allow me to leave you with a challenge to act upon what you have read to this point.

Assess your daily activity. Consider every deed you do, every thought you have. Is it aimed at shalom? Do you plan your work and your play and your rest in such a way that it enhances wholeness between yourself and the rest of God's creation? Do your daily activities bring you closer to God?

These are not just rhetorical questions. They are questions we must ask ourselves every day. As Kingdom members, we are part of God's mission. We must, therefore, be working toward shalom. It is, after all, our reason for existence, our goal, our mission statement.

Part Three -- God's Strategic Plan

Okay, so we've seen how being part of God's Kingdom is like being part of a well-run organization. We have before us a mission that guides our every activity and a vision for what the Kingdom will look like when we are all doing our part and achieve our (God's!) goals.

Let's consider how we implement the mission and vision. Put in organizational terms, let's look at the strategy we are to use.

Strategic Plan

Here, again, God has a goal: growth. This seems overly simplified and obvious. If you were to ask any organizational leader if they are looking for growth, you might get a dirty look of "isn't that the goal of every organization?" Well...not necessarily.

First, I know of organizations who do not want to grow so much as they want to meet the need they target. So, if the need grows, the organization grows, if the need diminishes, so does the work of the organization.

Take, for example, organizations that work to eradicate specific diseases. As cases increase, the organization grows to serve the need for more research, medication, treatment, facilities, etc. If, on the other hand, the organization is able to stem the tide on a particular disease, the need for their services decreases.

Second, there are organizations that do not want to grow — period.

I know of a church that hired a pastor to lead them in growth. He worked diligently reaching out to the community, inviting new folks into the congregation.

After several months of effort, but with little success, he was told by one of the church leaders that they did not approve of the "kinds of people" he was bringing into the church. When pressed, the leader admitted that he, and many others in the church, liked the church "just the way it is" and did not see a need for new people.

The church had become a social club. And they were a closed society. They did not want to grow.

Not surprisingly, the pastor decided to move on. In fitting irony, the church that had hired the pastor to help them grow, then pushed him out because they realized they did not, in fact, want to grow, closed shortly after the pastor's departure.

I am told by doctor friends that the human body is in a constant state of growth. Some of our bodies grow in different directions. Newborn babies grow into adults much too quickly for parents' comfort. In order to sustain life, the body must continually create new cells.

Think about it. How many times do you have to clip your nails? Why? Because the body is constantly creating more protection for the ends of your fingers and toes.

How often do you get a haircut? Why? Because the body is continually growing more hair (more for some of us than for others, admittedly).

Your bone marrow creates new blood cells. Your skin is constantly being replenished.

When your body stops doing these, and many, many other necessary cell replacement activities, it stops growing.

The body continues to grow – until it starts to die. The same is true, I believe for any organism: a business, a church, and God's Kingdom. The difference is that the Kingdom will never die.

Therefore, we can conclude, the Kingdom is in a constant state of growth. And that, my friends, has some serious implications for those of us who choose to be part of the Kingdom.

The Good News of the Parables

Numbers are very important in the Bible. They're used as symbols in the many stories and speeches found in both the Old and New Testaments.

For example, the number twelve was the number of perfection for the Jews. In Jewish tradition, rabbis taught students in groups of twelve. That's probably why Jesus chose twelve of his disciples to be his closest associates.

Another important number is three. The number three represents God. God is the trinity, the three-in-one. So when we read something that has three parts, or involves three things or persons we know that it is in some way related to God.

Another use of the number three: it is used by many writers in the Bible is to indicate a message from God. When one of the prophets wanted to make sure the people understood that his message was from God, he stated it three times.

Mark used this idea in his gospel, too. In chapter four we find three parables. And all three parables talk about the same thing. Therefore, we know that whatever those three parables say, together they have some important good news for us from God.

As we begin to look for the message we find a warning flag. As Jesus begins to tell these people his story he warns us to "listen!"

So now it should be pretty obvious we're about to hear some great good news. It is in fact some of the greatest good news in the Gospel of Mark. So let's find out what it is.

All three of these parables have an agricultural motif. Makes sense. Jesus lived in and addressed an agriculture society. These parables deal with the sowing, growth and results of seeds planted in the ground.

Three Parables

The first nine versus of Mark chapter four contain a parable with various names. Some have called it the Parable of the Sower. Others call it the Parable of the Soils.

> *"Listen! A sower went out to sow. And as he sowed, some seed fell along the path, and the birds came and devoured it. Other seed fell on rocky ground, where it did not have much soil, and immediately it sprang up, since it had no depth of soil. And when the sun rose, it*

was scorched, and since it had no root, it withered away. Other seed fell among thorns, and the thorns grew up and choked it, and it yielded no grain. And other seeds fell into good soil and produced grain, growing up and increasing and yielding thirtyfold and sixtyfold and a hundredfold."

Mark 4:3-8

In the story, we have a sower – a farmer – who is planting seeds. Now in Jesus' day farmers didn't have John Deere tractors and mechanical planting machines like we do.

No, they would begin the year by going out into the field and scattering seed on the ground by hand. They didn't plow the field or disk it or even put fertilizer on it. They just walked around an open unprepared field and slung seeds. After the seeds were distributed, the farmer would hitch the ox to a plow and turn the seed under.

Using this primitive method had its disadvantages of course. It meant that the plants would come up haphazard and make the harvest, which was done completely by hand, very difficult. They literally had to start on one end of the field and harvest the grain as they cleared a path.

This method also meant that not all of the seed would produce grain. Some of it would fall on the spaces that had been beaten down into a path. The oxen and farmers had to travel between their fields somehow. So they created paths simply by traveling the same path over and over again. Seeds that fell on this path were never turned under and the birds came and ate them.

Some of the seed fell on ground that was rocky. Farmers that have fields located in river bottoms may have the same problem. There just isn't enough soil there to do any good. The root system cannot take hold and get the nutrients to the plant. So when the hot sun comes up over the horizon, the plant literally burns up.

Some other seed fell on ground infested by thorn plants. You know as well as I do that the healthiest plants in the backyard garden are the ones that are not supposed to be there – weeds! And if you don't have any chemicals to get rid of the weeds, they will soon choke out the tomatoes and corn and beans and take over the whole garden. And because first century farmers had no chemicals to spray on the fields, it was inevitable that some of the seeds would sprout but then be choked out by the weeds.

But despite all these possibilities, some of the seed would fall on good, rich, deep soil. And come harvest time, the farmer could go out into the field and take in 30, 60 up to 100 times what he had sown in the spring. This kind of return at harvest time made all the risks worthwhile.

In the second parable Jesus tells us a little more about the farming practice in his time.

> "The kingdom of God is as if a man should scatter seed on the ground. He sleeps and rises night and day, and the seed sprouts and grows; he knows not how. The earth produces by itself, first the blade, then the ear, then the full grain in the ear. But when the grain is ripe, at once he puts in the sickle, because the harvest has come."

Mark 4:26-29

Again the process begins with a farmer who scatters seed on the unprepared ground. When he was done scattering the seed and plowing it under, his work was finished until harvest.

Oh, I imagine he probably built a scarecrow or two to keep the birds away. And he probably hired some of the local boys to bring their slingshots around every so often and chase off the wild animals. But that was about it.

There was no cultivating to do. No fertilizer to spread. It was futile to try and pull up all the weeds, so they were allowed to grow right along with the grain. But despite the inactivity of the farmer, seed sprouted and grew and produced grain.

The earth and God did all the work. It gave the seed what it needed to become a small blade of the plant. And then an ear of grain would appear and eventually the ear would be full of grain.

After the growth process had been completed, without any help from the farmer, it was harvest time. And again the farmer would go out and taking in 30, 60, up to 100 times what he had sown in the spring.

The third parable uses a little different comparison.

"With what can we compare the kingdom of God, or what parable shall we use for it? It is like a grain of mustard seed, which, when sown on the ground, is the smallest of all the seeds on earth, yet when it is sown it grows up and becomes larger than all the garden plants

and puts out large branches, so that the birds of the air can make nests in its shade."

Mark 4:30-32

This short story contains the same general ideas as the other two parables. Jesus very simply states the fact that the tiny mustard seed, when planted, grows up to be one of the largest plants in the field.

Nowadays we know that the mustard seed is not necessarily the absolute smallest seed we know of. Nor is the mustard plan the largest that we know of. But the illustration is a good one nonetheless. The large mustard plant has its beginning in a very tiny seed. From such a modest start comes very big results.

The Good News

NOW HAVE YOU BEEN LISTENING carefully? Have you discovered what the good news is? Let me help. At the beginning of the last two parables, Jesus says that the parables are being used to illustrate what? The Kingdom of God. So we know now that whatever the good news is, it tells us something about the Kingdom of God.

So now let's see what the main point is in these three parables. Whatever it is, we will surely find it in all three passages. So we can rule out the sower, or farmer first off. He appears only in the first two parables and is not even mentioned in the parable of the mustard seed.

The seed itself appears in all three parables. In fact the seed is the center of attention in the second parable and a very important feature of the third. But in the first parable, there is little emphasis on the seed. In the first parable, all the emphasis seems to be on the soil. But not so in the other two. So what do these three parables have in common? Results!

All three look at the end of the process -- the harvest. The Parable of the Mustard Seed tells us that the Kingdom, though it had small beginnings, will be the largest kingdom of all in the end. The parable of the seed growing on its own tells us that the Kingdom will grow and develop. Come harvest time, there will be a multitude of work for the Christians. And the so called Parable of the Soils tells us that despite all the possible problems, the Kingdom will bring in 30, 60 or even 100 times what was started and even expected.

As the seeds of the gospel are planted, some will fall on deaf ears. And those who reject the gospel will be destroyed by evil. Others will fall on ears which are somewhat receptive. Those people hear and respond to the gospel. They are excited about it for awhile. But they get tired of it quickly. They don't study their Bible. They don't go to church. They don't pray. They don't seek God's will for using their time, talent and treasure. And soon after, they will wither away and they too will disappear from the Kingdom.

And the gospel will be preached to some who will accept it and live it until the worldly attitudes of society creep up around them. These worldly attitudes will attract their attention and distract them from their life of faith. They grow and look like good Christians for a while, but they never do any good -- they never produce fruit.

But thanks to God, sometimes the gospel will come to good soil. Some people will receive it and happily accept it and live it and produce fruit because of it. And because of this good soil the Kingdom of God will have an unbelievable harvest. Perhaps, then, a better name for this illustration would be the Parable of the Great Harvest.

How would you like to get a 30-, 60- or 100-fold return on the seed you plant in your garden this spring? Better yet, how would you like to get a 30-, 60- or 100-fold return on the investment you put in the bank? Yes, that's a 3,000, 6,000 and 10,000 percent interest rate! I know it's not possible to get a 3,000, 6,000 or 10,000 percent interest rate at the bank. But I do know that it's possible when it comes to the Kingdom of God.

In fact, I can recite many examples where the great harvest is already being taken in. I would point to the largest church in the world in Seoul, South Korea, where tens of thousands worship every week. I would note the Crystal Cathedral in California. Say what you want about it, and despite its challenges, it started in Iowa with a man with a vision, his family, a car full of worldly possessions and a trailer hauling a church organ cross-country. Today, several thousand worship there.

I could talk about the many so-called mega churches we have in our world. Saddleback in California, Willow Creek in Chicago, Southeast Christian church in Louisville, Kentucky. I'm sure you can name many others.

The great harvest promised by Jesus in the parables is happening now. The harvest is upon us. The seed has been and is being sown, and God is giving it growth. Soon it will be our responsibility to go out into the field and take in the grain of the harvest. What can we do to prepare for it?

Preparing for the Harvest

BEFORE THE HARVEST, a farmer prepares the tools and himself for the work of harvest. Farmers don't just go out and start up the combine and drive it into the field. No, they get it out, repair it, oil and grease it and make adjustments so that, when they get in the field, the harvest will be smooth and without interruption.

So, too, must we prepare for the harvest. We have to prepare ourselves. We have to put on our work clothes and make sure we're in the right state of mind and in good physical condition -- in good spiritual condition, as well.

We have to prepare to work in the harvest expecting a great harvest. If we go about our work in the church saying it's not going to make any difference – it won't. If we don't think inviting people to church will get them to come – it won't. If we think our efforts won't make any difference –

they won't. If we think our small church cannot do great things – it never will. But it can!

If several workers are harvesting in the same field they have to be working together. They have to be organized to know what to do next. And if they disagree with one another, they must come to some sort of an agreement before they start to work. If they don't, they could damage the machinery, or they could hurt themselves and they can surely lose a lot of grain and not get the job done it all.

Likewise, in preparing for harvest in the church, we may disagree on how and what and when and where we're going to do things. But we have to reach an agreement before we start, or else we will fail to do God's work as he wants it done. This is what Paul talks about when he speaks of unity in the Church.

We also have to prepare the equipment for the harvest. That means we have to make sure we have all the necessary programs, facilities and people to do the job.

Look about your church. What programs and materials and facilities are being used well? What leaders are doing an exceptional job?

If you look hard enough, you will find many examples of the right people doing the right things at the right time with the right programs and the right materials. They are workers in the harvest and the harvest is great.

In three parables Jesus tells us the Kingdom of God is coming in a great harvest. We see all around us examples of how the great harvest is already beginning and how we are experiencing the blessings of an abundant harvest in the Kingdom of God. And we see examples in our own church of the programs and the people and the resources being used effectively in the harvest of the Kingdom.

These three parables should be enough to make it obvious to us the good news of the parables. The Kingdom of God is near and it's going to be a great harvest. When it arrives, we must be ready. So as Jesus said, listen and get ready!

Parable of the Talents

There is, however, another parable that we must consider. It is the very familiar, but very difficult Parable of the Talents.

Now, before we get too far down the road, let me reveal one of my pet peeves (I have several!). I have heard far too many sermons using this parable to talk about personal talents/skills/gifts. This parable is not about the abilities God has given to us.

There are many passages that anyone can study and discuss to discover how God has gifted us, and how he intends for us to use those gifts. But Jesus was not addressing spiritual gifts in this parable.

Rather, this parable is all about what it means to be a participant in the Kingdom. It is all about our responsibilities and God's expectations of us as we seek to accomplish his will in creation. And it has some very serious implications!

> "For it will be like a man going on a journey, who called his servants and entrusted to them his property. To one he gave five talents, to another two, to another one, to each according to his ability. Then he went away.
>
> *Matthew 25:14-15*

In this parable, we have a master of an estate who assigns responsibility for the care of his estate to three servants. Now, this should sound very familiar to anyone who is part of God's Kingdom.

This scenario is exactly what happened in creation. God, the creator and master of the estate took all that he created and entrusted it to his stewards. Originally, of course, that was Adam and Eve. But the assignment was to all of humanity.

As Christians, we are servants of God and are responsible for the care of God's estate.

Back to the parable...

> *He who had received the five talents went at once and traded with them, and he made five talents more. So also he who had the two talents made two talents more. But he who had received the one talent went and dug in the ground and hid his master's money. Now after a long time the master of those servants came and settled accounts with them. And he who had received the five talents came forward, bringing five talents more, saying, 'Master, you delivered to me five talents; here I have made five talents more.' His master said to him, 'Well done, good and faithful servant. You have been faithful over a little; I will set you over much. Enter into the joy*

of your master.' And he also who had the two talents came forward, saying, 'Master, you delivered to me two talents; here I have made two talents more.' His master said to him, 'Well done, good and faithful servant. You have been faithful over a little; I will set you over much. Enter into the joy of your master.' He also who had received the one talent came forward, saying, 'Master, I knew you to be a hard man, reaping where you did not sow, and gathering where you scattered no seed, so I was afraid, and I went and hid your talent in the ground. Here you have what is yours.'

Matthew 25:16-25

The three servants are each given shares of the estate to care for. Note that each is given "according to his ability." This is important – keep it in mind!

Each takes what he is assigned and manages it in his own way. When the master returns, each steward reports his results to the master.

Two have had considerable success, one has not.

The two who realized success actually doubled the shares of their master's estate that they were given. We do not know exactly what they did to double their shares.

Perhaps they invested in similar way to how we invest in the stock market today. Perhaps they used the resources to barter for other, more valuable resources.

It is not important how they did it. What is important is that they accomplished what the master expected of them.

The third servant was more conservative. He did not invest, or follow the example of the other two servants. He simply hid his shares in the ground so as not to lose any of his master's estate.

Now, we are told that each was given according to his ability. So, obviously, this fellow was not as capable as the other two servants. Can we blame him for doing what he did? The master did!

> *"You wicked and slothful servant! You knew that I reap where I have not sown and gather where I scattered no seed? Then you ought to have invested my money with the bankers, and at my coming I should have received what was my own with interest. So take the talent from him and give it to him who has the ten talents. For to everyone who has will more be given, and he will have an abundance. But from the one who has not, even what he has will be taken away. And cast the worthless servant into the outer darkness. In that place there will be weeping and gnashing of teeth."*
>
> **Matthew 25:26-30**

I must admit that, for years, I felt sorry for this fellow. Every time I read the parable, I just never understood why the master came down so hard on the man. Okay, maybe he shows disappointment that the servant did not gain anything. But what did he expect? He knew this man was a bit dimmer than the other two.

Yet the punishment is pretty severe. He is thrown into the outer darkness. He is excommunicated from the estate – kicked out on the street. Poor guy.

What is Jesus trying to tell us in this parable?

Don't lose sight of the fact that Jesus' parable is about the Kingdom. As we have just seen, the Kingdom is all about growth. The servants in this parable knew that. They knew what was expected of them. Their master expected his estate to grow while he was away.

The third servant says as much. "I knew you were a hard man." That is, I knew what you expected of me. I know what it means to be part of your estate. We know what it means to be part of God's Kingdom. We know that the Kingdom is all about growth.

Yet the servant refused to participate. Some may say, "Well, he really just failed in his efforts." Read carefully, that is not true. He did not try. He knew that he was expected to grow his allotment of the estate, but he did not even try to do so.

He refused to participate in what he knew the master expected – growth of the estate. So it is no wonder that he was thrown out!

Such is the fate of any and all who refuse to participate in the Kingdom.

Now, this may strike fear in our hearts and minds. If I am expected to invest and grow my little corner of the Kingdom, but don't, will I be thrown into the outer darkness?

Remember that the punishment of the third servant was not due to his failure, but due to his refusal. If we accept our role and are faithful in serving according to what we know is God's will, we will be found faithful.

In his letter to the Corinthian church, we are told by Paul, "Moreover, it is required of stewards that they be found trustworthy." (I Corinthians 4:2)

Perhaps you have heard Mother Theresa's adage, "We are not called to be successful, we are called to be faithful."

If, therefore, we accept our role and God's call, if we give it our best shot, yet fail, God will judge, not by our results, but by our effort. It is when we know what is expected, but refuse to participate, that God looks at our results and finds us lacking.

Part Four -- God's Tactics

Now let's look at the Kingdom in terms of tactics. Tactics are the day-to-day activities which, in very practical ways, make the strategy come to life.

As noted in the Acknowledgements, I discovered a pattern that repeats itself throughout the Bible. A pattern within the scriptures through which I believe God speaks to us today. A pattern that is very telling as we go about our, or should I say God's business in the Kingdom.

The Pattern

THE PATTERN IS READILY APPARENT, as noted in the story shared earlier. Most anyone can find it in the scriptures. This is not surprising to me. What is surprising is that no one to date has shared this pattern – at least not in such a way as to suggest that it is a dominant and significant pattern throughout both the Old and New Testaments.

The pattern is so dominant throughout the scriptures that I believe it must be a revelation of how God seeks to work. This, then, is what I believe to be God's tactical plan for life in the Kingdom.

Before looking at some examples of the pattern in scripture, I will briefly outline it. Then we will consider several examples of the pattern as it occurs in the scriptures. Finally, we will consider the "so what factor" (as a friend and co-worker calls it). We will talk about why this pattern is important to us as members of God's Kingdom.

The pattern is a rather simple one. As noted earlier, it is one that is repeated at various levels – short stories, parables, biographies, even whole books – throughout the Bible.

I believe God inspired the pattern to show us how we should operate on a daily basis as members of his Kingdom.

The pattern, briefly stated, is: Need, Resources, Application, Results.

To explain...

*I*n a given passage, early in the situation, we read about or discover a need. It may be a need for food (fairly common). It may be an enemy that is persecuting God's people (very common). It may be a bit more obscure, as we will see later.

Once the need is called to attention, a process of identifying the available resources begins. The resources needed to meet the need vary from incident-to-incident. The available resources depend upon the situation – what the need is, location, etc. The resources include both material possessions and human resources, as well as others we will find along the way.

When the resources are identified, they are then applied in such a way that they meet the need. Humanity acts, food is distributed, God supplies.

Finally, and most importantly, we read about abundant results. The results always exceed the original need. They are always a result of God's activity. They are always, as we should expect, abundant.

The Feeding of the 5,000

THE BEST AND MOST OBVIOUS example of the pattern is the familiar story of Jesus feeding the 5,000. This is the story which first sparked my discovery of the pattern – perhaps because the pattern is so apparent in the text.

The story is found in the gospel of Mark. The setting is a remote place – probably on or near the Sea of Galilee. The miracle is repeated in Gentile territory, as well, with similar results, and is related in all the gospels. We will consider the story as related in the Gospel of Mark, chapter six.

Need

> The apostles returned to Jesus and told him all that they had done and taught. And he said to them, "Come away by yourselves to a desolate place and rest a while." For many were coming and going, and they had no leisure

even to eat. And they went away in the boat to a desolate place by themselves. Now many saw them going and recognized them, and they ran there on foot from all the towns and got there ahead of them. When he went ashore he saw a great crowd, and he had compassion on them, because they were like sheep without a shepherd. And he began to teach them many things.

Mark 6:30-34

It's interesting that the day did not go at all as Jesus had intended. He had told his disciples, "Let's get away and go someplace where we can be by ourselves."

But Jesus' popularity had grown so much by this time that crowds of people followed his every move. So, when he and the twelve got into a boat and started rowing, people saw them, the word spread, and they followed along the shore.

This is not a difficult task. While I have never visited the area, I understand that the Sea of Galilee is comparatively small. You can see the other side from anywhere along the shore.

So it was easy for the crowd to follow along. Eventually, it became apparent to the crowd where Jesus' entourage was going. For we read in the story that they "went on ahead" and settled in before Jesus and his crew arrived.

And, apparently, the word had spread, for, when Jesus arrived, there was already a large crowd of people.

And, when Jesus saw the crowd, he "had compassion on them for they were like sheep without a shepherd."

Now, as we consider the needs, let's not skip to the big miracle. Let's pause here a moment and consider all the needs.

Let's think, first, about the implications of sheep needing a shepherd. Sheep, as I understand it, are not particularly intelligent beasts. They are not able to fend for themselves. If left alone, they will die.

Sheep need a shepherd to protect them. In the fields where they graze, there are dangers. Wild animals, predators, will attack. If unprotected, poachers will try to steal them.

Jesus may have seen this need in the people who were being misled by the religious leaders of the day. The teachings of the Pharisees and Sadducees were intended to keep the crowds under the control of these religious leaders. They were not particularly good shepherds – they protected their own interests rather than the leading people to God.

Sheep will wander off if not herded. That's why sheep dogs are such valuable possessions of farmers who keep sheep. And, if they wander off, they need to be rescued. Such, again, was the need of the crowd.

Very early in my theological education, I learned the very practical lessons of the shepherd's staff. Much more than a walking stick to support the shepherd, the blunt end of the staff is used as a weapon to fight off enemies. The hooked end is used to reach and redirect wandering sheep.

They were wandering, not knowing that the religious leaders where misleading them. They were not close to God because no one had shown them the way to be close to God.

One other feature of the shepherd's staff I learned – the blunt end can also be used to prod sheep along when they need to move. Such is especially the case when the shepherd needs to move the herd to a better location for grazing. This is, perhaps, the most important reason a herd needs a shepherd – food.

Which brings us to the most obvious need of the crowd...

And when it grew late, his disciples came to him and said, "This is a desolate place, and the hour is now late. Send them away to go into the surrounding countryside and villages and buy themselves something to eat."

Mark 6:35-36

Along about sunset, as I picture it, everyone was getting tired and hungry. I find it interesting that the disciples came to Jesus as if he did not notice the fatigue of the crowd. If he is truly the Good Shepherd, he already knew their need.

I also find it interesting that the disciples pointed out the fatigue and hunger of the crowd. They did not acknowledge their own needs. Perhaps we can take this as selflessness on their part. "Our needs are not important, but this crowd really needs food."

I tend to think, however, that they were simply ashamed to call attention to their own needs – unwilling to admit that they were tired and hungry, too. Don't we all want to be thought of as tireless, selfless servants of God?!

We hate to admit our mistakes, our lack of expertise, our weaknesses. Yet, of all people, God knows our shortcomings and is readily available to meet them.

Resources

*T*he disciples brought the need of the crowd to the attention of Jesus. Isn't it interesting that they came to the very best resource they had...but did not realize it!

Rather than asking Jesus to feed them, they suggested he send them away to the surrounding villages to find their own food.

Here, Jesus turns the tables.

But he answered them, "You give them something to eat." And they said to him, "Shall we go and buy two hundred denarii worth of bread and give it to them to eat?"

Mark 6:37

They came to him with a need for sustenance. They did not ask him (who was most able to help) to meet the need. So, he told them, "You give them something to eat."

Now someone in the group was quite adept at math. For they quickly calculated that it would take a year's salary to feed the large crowd. And, of course, they did not have access to such a sizable resource.

Rather than assessing the available resources, the disciples were focused on the need. Sometimes the need is so great that we cannot take our eyes off of it.

When cancer strikes, we can only think of the worst case scenario – how long do I have? We jump to the conclusion without asking about the prognosis, the possible treatments and the potential for a cure.

When the bills are stacked so high we cannot see across the kitchen table, we file for bankruptcy rather than looking at all the possible alternatives for fulfilling our obligations.

But if the need is to be met, we must take an assessment of the resources God has provided to meet the needs – no matter how meager.

And he said to them, "How many loaves do you have? Go and see." And when they had found out, they said, "Five, and two fish."

Matthew 6:38

Jesus redirected the disciples attention away from the need. He told them, in essence, "I don't care what you don't have, tell me what you do have."

I suspect there was what we call in Indiana, some "hem-hawing around." They were tired, they were hungry, Jesus had promised them a day off, they wanted to move on.

Nonetheless, they wandered about the crowd asking, "Who has food they are willing to share?"

In the Gospel of John, it is interesting to note who comes up with the necessary resources. Of all the people gathered there, only one young boy was willing to share what he had.

I cannot imagine that one young boy was the only one there with any food. Remember, they are in a remote place. And while there was a certain spur-of-the-moment excitement about the opportunity to hear and meet Jesus the famous prophet, surely some planned ahead and grabbed some food before chasing after Jesus' entourage.

And I cannot believe that, among a crowd of 15,000 to 20,000 (there were 5,000 men, not counting the women and children) there were only 2 loaves of bread and five fish. There had to be hundreds of Jewish mothers in the crowd. Can you imagine they did not have something with them to pacify the kids (and men!) while they were gone for the day?!

Many, of course, were poor and did not have the resources to buy food on short notice. So the need, and the impending fulfillment of the need, was, beyond a doubt, miraculous for such a large crowd.

The boy probably did not realize he did not have enough to feed the crowd. Either that, or he knew Jesus could do anything he wanted with whatever he had to offer.

The Bible says, "A little child shall lead them." No wonder Jesus loved children so much. No wonder he tells us to become like children. For, with such faith, he can meet any need – even feeding a huge flock of sheep with five loaves and two fish.

Now some who discount this miracle say that the little boy simply inspired the adults to share what they brought. As noted earlier, it is hard to fathom that no one else in such a vast crowd had food with them, no matter how meager.

I do believe it is possible that the boy's generosity inspired others to share. This, in itself, is miraculous – how one young boy can inspire a multitude to share their resources. I've been a pastor. I know how hard it is to inspire a congregation to share!

But, if that, indeed, is the case, it is only a small part of the miracle. Jesus is the focus of the miracle. It is he who brought the available resources to bear on the great need set before him. It is he who wants his disciples (both then and now) to realize that he is our source for sustenance – not just in the remote places, but in every place we find ourselves every day of our lives.

Application

> *Then he commanded them all to sit down in groups on the green grass. So they sat down in groups, by hundreds and by fifties. And taking the five loaves and the two fish he looked up to heaven and said a blessing and broke the loaves and gave them to the disciples to set before the people. And he divided the two fish among them all.*
>
> **Mark 6:39-41**

We cannot look at this section of the story without acknowledging some additional resources that are added into the mix. Note that Jesus organized the crows into smaller groups. In the Gospel of Luke, we read that Jesus told his disciples to divide the crowd into groups of about 50.

Sometimes needs are so great that they appear to be insurmountable. In God's view, nothing is impossible. Jesus simply broke the need down into manageable portions. Looking at groups of 50 made the resources look a little more valuable.

Jesus also applied the most powerful resource of all. Before he distributed the loaves and fish, he took them in hand, looked to his Father and asked God's blessing on what he was about to do.

How often do we fail to acknowledge God as the source of all we need? How often do we fail to ask God to bless and be involved in what we are doing to meet needs around us? When we fail to do so, we are neglecting the most powerful and important resource at our disposal.

It is not a magic bullet. We dare not ask God to bless some scatter-brained plan we have come up with on our own. Prayer must cover all our plans – from beginning to end. And when we invite God into our plans, seeking his will, participation and blessing, the results are abundant.

Results

> And they all ate and were satisfied. And they took up twelve baskets full of broken pieces and of the fish. And those who ate the loaves were five thousand men.
>
> ***Mark 6:42-44***

*T*hey all ate and all were satisfied! Again, there had to be some 15,000 to 20,000 people there that day. I figure, for each man, there was probably a wife and maybe a child or two. Granted, there were some single men, but there were also widows and orphans. Calculating one woman and one child for every man brings us to a total of 15,000 – minimum!

And <u>all</u> ate and <u>all</u> were satisfied. They didn't just get a taste. They all ate until they were full.

Now, the most amazing result...

When they were done, they collected twelve baskets full of leftovers. They ended with more than what they had when they started! When we turn to God – our best resource – we have plenty to meet the need and more left over for next time!

THE STORY OF JOSEPH

LET'S LOOK AT ANOTHER EXAMPLE of the recurring pattern – this one from the Old Testament. Let's see how God's Kingdom tactics are applied in the story of Joseph.

The story of Joseph is found in the last several chapters of Genesis. Here, again, we see the familiar repeating patterned of need, resources, application and results. In this comparatively long story, however, it's a bit more difficult to discern each aspect of the pattern.

So let's take a look and see what we find.

Need

We're going to jump into the middle of the story. We'll look at some of the early-story details momentarily, but, in sum...

Joseph, the bratty youngest son of Jacob, shows off his ability to interpret dreams by telling his brothers that they will, eventually, bow down to him. His brothers are ticked off to the point that they want to kill him. Instead, they sell him into slavery and he winds up in Egypt.

Being the clever and intelligent young man that he is, he lands on his feet in Potiphar's court. There he serves wisely, but is framed by Potiphar's wife on sexual harassment charges and lands in prison.

There his dream interpretation skills pay off (this time for the better!). He tells Pharaoh that seven years of bounty will be followed by seven years of famine. He boldly advises Pharaoh regarding strategy for dealing with the impending time of need. Pharaoh rewards Joseph by making him second-in-command.

Joseph begins implementing the plan he suggested. There we pick up the story...

> *The seven years of plenty that occurred in the land of Egypt came to an end, and the seven years of famine began to come, as Joseph had said. There was famine in all lands, but in all the land of Egypt there was bread. When all the land of Egypt was famished, the people cried to Pharaoh for bread. Pharaoh said to all the Egyptians, "Go to Joseph. What he says to you, do."*
>
> *So when the famine had spread over all the land, Joseph opened all the storehouses and sold to the Egyptians, for the famine was severe in the land of Egypt. Moreover, all the earth came to Egypt to Joseph to buy grain, because the famine was severe over all the earth.*

Genesis 41:53-57

Can the need be more obvious? Famine – everywhere. The text speaks specifically of the situation in Egypt, but makes it very clear that the famine affected all the earth. So the need, of course, is for food. There is a famine in all the land.

There is a more important, underlying need, however. Famine endangers the people living in the area affected. It includes therefore the Egyptians as well as people living in the surrounding area. Included in these peoples of the surrounding area is Joseph and his family.

And who are Joseph and his family? The Israelites. The people of promise. The great nation that God promised to Abraham earlier in Genesis.

So the need is not just for food to feed the general population in the area at the time. The need is for food to feed Israel as well. The need is to save the nation of Israel. To ensure the fulfillment of God's promise of a future great nation.

Resources

> When Jacob learned that there was grain for sale in Egypt, he said to his sons, "Why do you look at one another?" And he said, "Behold, I have heard that there is grain for sale in Egypt. Go down and buy grain for us there, that we may live and not die."
>
> **Genesis 42:1-2**

My daughter is always hungry. She comes to me all the time saying, "I'm hungry." I always tell her, "There's a cure for that." She rolls her eyes and leaves me alone.

The cure for hunger is food. The resources needed to relieve the Egyptian famine are very obvious – food, specifically grain. Back in Canaan, where the famine is even worse, Jacob knows where to find the cure.

But let's not overlook the two most important resources in any of the stories we are considering. Never overlook the human resources that are available.

In this story we have to look at Joseph as the primary human resource that God uses to relieve the famine. And, of course, we must never overlook God himself and his power as he intervenes to meet the need.

Application of Resources

Now the application of resources is rather long and drawn out. In fact, the application of resources starts before anyone ever realizes the need. The application begins even before the famine is foreseen by Joseph.

To see how God applies the resource of Joseph to the need, we have to look all the way back to the beginning of the story of Joseph. In Genesis chapter 37 we are introduced to Joseph:

> *Joseph, being seventeen years old, was pasturing the flock with his brothers. He was a boy with the sons of*

> *Bilhah and Zilpah, his father's wives. And Joseph brought a bad report of them to their father. Now Israel loved Joseph more than any other of his sons, because he was the son of his old age. And he made him a robe of many colors. But when his brothers saw that their father loved him more than all his brothers, they hated him and could not speak peacefully to him.*
>
> ***Genesis 37:2-4***

Here we read that Joseph "brought a bad report" to his father about his older brothers. That is, Joseph was "telling" on his brothers. Joseph was a "tattle-tale," as we would say today.

As we continue to read the story, we find out that he was also given special gifts and skills by God. He was able to interpret dreams. That in itself is not a bad thing. But Joseph used his special gifts to lord it over his brothers.

> *Now Joseph had a dream, and when he told it to his brothers they hated him even more. He said to them, "Hear this dream that I have dreamed: Behold, we were binding sheaves in the field, and behold, my sheaf arose and stood upright. And behold, your sheaves gathered around it and bowed down to my sheaf." His brothers said to him, "Are you indeed to reign over us? Or are you indeed to rule over us?" So they hated him even more for his dreams and for his words.*
>
> *Then he dreamed another dream and told it to his brothers and said, "Behold, I have dreamed another dream. Behold, the sun, the moon, and eleven stars were bowing down to me." But when he told it to his father*

> and to his brothers, his father rebuked him and said to him, "What is this dream that you have dreamed? Shall I and your mother and your brothers indeed come to bow ourselves to the ground before you?" And his brothers were jealous of him, but his father kept the saying in mind.
>
> ### Genesis 37:5-11

So Joseph was a tattle-tale, a dreamer, and rather full of himself – especially considering he was the younger brother. He was a little too big for his britches as we might say today. To be blunt, Joseph was a brat!

You can imagine how all this went over with his older brothers. Actually, you don't have to imagine, you can read it for yourself again. "They hated him even more." "And his brothers were jealous of him." They became irate to the point they were ready to kill him.

But thank goodness for oldest brother Reuben. He was the oldest – quite a bit older than Joseph – and obviously considerably wiser and more levelheaded than his brothers. He convinced his brothers to spare Joseph's life.

So the brothers threw Joseph into an old dry well. I suspect they intended just to leave him there for dead. But fortuitously, a caravan of Ishmaelite traders came by.

Now this was not unusual. In the land were Joseph and his brothers lived there were trade routes frequented by caravans of traders such as the one that happened by. It would not have been unusual to see such trade caravans passing by on occasion.

And as the caravan passed by, the brothers decided, rather than kill their brother Joseph they would sell him into slavery. Make a little money for themselves and pass it off as an unfortunate death to their father Jacob.

Let me pause here in the story and raise a flag for you to watch for in the story. Watch how God works throughout this whole story. In a series of twists and turns, some very fortunate, others not so much so, Joseph winds up as the overseer in the house of Potiphar.

The Lord was with Joseph, and he became a successful man, and he was in the house of his Egyptian master. His master saw that the Lord was with him and that the Lord caused all that he did to succeed in his hands. So Joseph found favor in his sight and attended him, and he made him overseer of his house and put him in charge of all that he had.

Genesis 39:2-4

God works in this rather circuitous story to relieve the famine that, to this point in the narrative, we know nothing about. We have the advantage of knowing where this story is going. It gives us a great view of what and how God works to bring about the very best out of even the worst situations. Watch and learn!

Just when it looks like things are on the upswing for Joseph, a series of less-than- fortunate events take place. Twists and turns that keep us on the edge of our seat. The stuff good movies are made of. I have often wondered why the story of Joseph has never been made into a motion picture. The plot line is filled with intrigue and suspense.

There is plenty left for the final reel and it turns out to be a real tear-jerker!

While in the service of Potiphar, Joseph is accused of rape by Potiphar's wife. Being a slave, he has no chance against a very powerful woman. His word against the ruler's wife's word – no brainer, the woman is right. Joseph is thrown in prison.

Here again, however, we see how God has laid out a plan and is using the resources he put in place before Joseph was even born. Remember that special gift that got Joseph in trouble with his brothers? Now it's going to get him out of a pit rather than in one! Well, at least in God's time.

In chapter 40 of Genesis, we read an interesting episode between Joseph and two strategically-placed cell mates. It seems the chief cupbearer and the chief baker of Pharaoh himself offended their master one day. And, not surprisingly, he threw them in jail – as overbearing tyrants often do.

Joseph, lucky man that he was (?), is told to take care of them. You see, Joseph was a blue-collar criminal, the cupbearer and baker were white-collar criminals.

And one night they both dreamed -- the cupbearer and the baker of the king of Egypt, who were confined in the prison -- each his own dream, and each dream with its own interpretation. When Joseph came to them in the morning, he saw that they were troubled. So he asked Pharaoh's officers who were with him in custody in his master's house, "Why are your faces downcast today?" They said to him, "We have had dreams, and there is no one to interpret them." And Joseph said to them, "Do not interpretations belong to God? Please tell them to me."

So the chief cupbearer told his dream to Joseph and said to him, "In my dream there was a vine before me, and on the vine there were three branches. As soon as it budded, its blossoms shot forth, and the clusters ripened into grapes. Pharaoh's cup was in my hand, and I took the grapes and pressed them into Pharaoh's cup and placed the cup in Pharaoh's hand." Then Joseph said to him, "This is its interpretation: the three branches are three days. In three days Pharaoh will lift up your head and restore you to your office, and you shall place Pharaoh's cup in his hand as formerly, when you were his cupbearer. Only remember me, when it is well with you, and please do me the kindness to mention me to Pharaoh, and so get me out of this house. For I was indeed stolen out of the land of the Hebrews, and here also I have done nothing that they should put me into the pit.

When the chief baker saw that the interpretation was favorable, he said to Joseph, "I also had a dream: there were three cake baskets on my head, and in the uppermost basket there were all sorts of baked food for Pharaoh, but the birds were eating it out of the basket on my head." And Joseph answered and said, "This is its interpretation: the three baskets are three days. In three days Pharaoh will lift up your head—from you!—and hang you on a tree. And the birds will eat the flesh from you."

> On the third day, which was Pharaoh's birthday, he made a feast for all his servants and lifted up the head of the chief cupbearer and the head of the chief baker among his servants. He restored the chief cupbearer to his position, and he placed the cup in Pharaoh's hand. But he hanged the chief baker, as Joseph had interpreted to them.
>
> ***Genesis 40:5-22***

Just a word for all the chief bakers out there. Be careful what you ask for. Good news for one is not necessarily good news for all. When the baker heard the good interpretation of the cupbearer's dream, he assumed his would be good news, as well. But, as we read, sometimes when you stick your neck out, you get hanged!

But Joseph saw opportunity knocking and he grabbed it. Unfortunately, we read the last little verse at the end of this episode: "Yet the chief cupbearer did not remember Joseph, but forgot him."

How sad. Just when it looks like our hero will be saved, his so-called friends fail him. The cupbearer forgot him – for two whole years.

We talk about the patience of Job. I think we overlook the patience of Joseph. The test says that he was 17 when he provoked his brothers to anger and 30 when he was reunited. Thirteen years. That's a long time to have to wait for God to work his will.

We've all had situations in our lives where, trusting in God for his answer to our fervent prayers for provision, healing, forgiveness, restitution, we have had to wait patiently. We don't like it. Sometimes our patience wears quite thin. But God's will works surely, and completely, in his time, not ours.

Joseph was patient. And his patience eventually paid off.

For, one day, Pharaoh had a dream!

Pharaoh dreamed that he was standing by the Nile, and behold, there came up out of the Nile seven cows attractive and plump, and they fed in the reed grass. And behold, seven other cows, ugly and thin, came up out of the Nile after them, and stood by the other cows on the bank of the Nile. And the ugly, thin cows ate up the seven attractive, plump cows. And Pharaoh awoke. And he fell asleep and dreamed a second time. And behold, seven ears of grain, plump and good, were growing on one stalk. And behold, after them sprouted seven ears, thin and blighted by the east wind. And the thin ears swallowed up the seven plump, full ears. And Pharaoh awoke, and behold, it was a dream. So in the morning his spirit was troubled, and he sent and called for all the magicians of Egypt and all its wise men. Pharaoh told them his dreams, but there was none who could interpret them to Pharaoh.

Then the chief cupbearer said to Pharaoh, "I remember my offenses today. When Pharaoh was angry with his servants and put me and the chief baker in custody in the house of the captain of the guard, we dreamed on the same night, he and I, each having a dream with its own interpretation. A young Hebrew was there with us, a servant of the captain of the guard.

> When we told him, he interpreted our dreams to us, giving an interpretation to each man according to his dream. And as he interpreted to us, so it came about. I was restored to my office, and the baker was hanged."
>
> **Genesis 41:1-13**

Thank goodness for long-term memory. Or maybe God at work in the mind of the cupbearer!?

So Joseph is summoned to the court of Pharaoh himself. Now, Joseph is still a slave and a prisoner, but my how the lowly have arisen! He finds himself in the office of the most powerful man on the earth in his day.

My goodness how God has orchestrated all this! Joseph stands in the presence of, perhaps, the only person alive who has the power to do something about the, as yet unforeseen famine.

> And Pharaoh said to Joseph, "I have had a dream, and there is no one who can interpret it. I have heard it said of you that when you hear a dream you can interpret it." Joseph answered Pharaoh, "It is not in me; God will give Pharaoh a favorable answer." Then Pharaoh said to Joseph, "Behold, in my dream I was standing on the banks of the Nile. Seven cows, plump and attractive, came up out of the Nile and fed in the reed grass. Seven other cows came up after them, poor and very ugly and thin, such as I had never seen in all the land of Egypt. And the thin, ugly cows ate up the first seven plump cows, but when they had eaten them no one would have known that they had eaten them, for they were still as

ugly as at the beginning. Then I awoke. I also saw in my dream seven ears growing on one stalk, full and good. Seven ears, withered, thin, and blighted by the east wind, sprouted after them, and the thin ears swallowed up the seven good ears. And I told it to the magicians, but there was no one who could explain it to me."

Then Joseph said to Pharaoh, "The dreams of Pharaoh are one; God has revealed to Pharaoh what he is about to do. The seven good cows are seven years, and the seven good ears are seven years; the dreams are one. The seven lean and ugly cows that came up after them are seven years, and the seven empty ears blighted by the east wind are also seven years of famine. It is as I told Pharaoh; God has shown to Pharaoh what he is about to do. There will come seven years of great plenty throughout all the land of Egypt, but after them there will arise seven years of famine, and all the plenty will be forgotten in the land of Egypt. The famine will consume the land, and the plenty will be unknown in the land by reason of the famine that will follow, for it will be very severe. And the doubling of Pharaoh's dream means that the thing is fixed by God, and God will shortly bring it about.

Genesis 41:15-32

But now we discover Joseph has yet another gift.

Now therefore let Pharaoh select a discerning and wise man, and set him over the land of Egypt. Let Pharaoh proceed to appoint overseers over the land and take one-fifth of the produce of the land of Egypt during the seven plentiful years. And let them gather all the food of these

> good years that are coming and store up grain under the authority of Pharaoh for food in the cities, and let them keep it. That food shall be a reserve for the land against the seven years of famine that are to occur in the land of Egypt, so that the land may not perish through the famine."
>
> **Genesis 41:33-36**

Not only can he interpret dreams, he has the biblical gift named in the New Testament as the gift of administration. And, here again, Joseph seizes the moment. He boldly suggests to Pharaoh a plan of action, even suggesting that someone...someone wise and discerning... hmmmmm... who could that be?

Joseph very wisely creates a plan to store up food in the seven years of plenty. He carefully selects storehouses in strategically located cities around the Egypt. In those storehouses he stores grain that will be used in the time of famine that is yet to come.

And the results, as usual, were exceedingly abundant...

Results

> *And Joseph went out from the presence of Pharaoh and went through all the land of Egypt. During the seven plentiful years the earth produced abundantly, and he gathered up all the food of these seven years, which occurred in the land of Egypt, and put the food in the cities. He put in every city the food from the fields around it. And Joseph stored up grain in great*

abundance, like the sand of the sea, until he ceased to measure it, for it could not be measured.

Genesis 41:46b-49

Yes, there was so much grain stored up that the famine, which came just as Joseph had interpreted, was weathered by the Egyptians. And, I think, we can assume all the land.

The basic need of food was met – in abundance. But the need to save Israel, the nation of promise, was fulfilled as well.

We know, as the late Paul Harvey would say, the rest of the story. We know about the reconciliation of Joseph and his brothers. We know that they brought their father, Jacob, to Egypt to live out his life.

And it was in Egypt that the Israelite nation grew in abundance. Not only was the family saved, it was brought into a place where it thrived. Even, as we read in Exodus, in a state of oppressive slavery.

Exodus 1:7 states: "...the people of Israel were fruitful and increased greatly; they multiplied and grew exceedingly strong, so that the land was filled with them."

God sees and anticipates. He knows the gifts and resources that he has ordained each of us to have. He grants them to be used for his will, not for us to lord over others. Yet even when we abuse the gifts and resources he bestows on us, he continues to work though our circumstances – the ones we bring on ourselves, the ones others bear upon us and the ones God himself sets before us.

It is important, therefore, that we acknowledge God, his gifts, his work in and among us. That we work with him, not against him, seeking his will, not ours. Taking advantage of the opportunities he sets before us and using our gifts to his glory. All the time knowing that hen God works in us and through us – even when it seems to take forever to get to fulfillment of his will – the results are always abundant!

Jesus' First Miracle

A WEDDING AT GALILEE provides an interesting backdrop for Jesus' first miracle. It also reveals the repeating pattern we have seen elsewhere.

On the third day there was a wedding at Cana in Galilee, and the mother of Jesus was there. Jesus also was invited to the wedding with his disciples.

John 2:1-2

Need

One fact we need to remember about Jesus: he had a Jewish mother. One that not even the Son of God could refuse.

Jewish weddings were quite the social event. The wedding celebration lasted seven days. It was the bride's family's responsibility to provide food and beverage for the entire celebration.

Typically, and in order to be frugal, the host would purchase expensive wine for the first few days of the event. After several days, the party-goers' discernment would be somewhat impaired. At that point, cheaper wine would be brought out – no one would know the difference.

Sounds practical, if not cheap. But no one would complain – every wedding host did it that way. What was really embarrassing was when the host ran out of wine completely.

Such was the case at the wedding in Galilee. Evidently, Mary, Jesus' mother, had some relationship with the bride's family. For, when she found out that the wine was gone, rather than starting gossip or even simply excusing herself politely and leaving, she decided to help before anyone noticed.

Resources

> When the wine ran out, the mother of Jesus said to him, "They have no wine."
>
> **John 2:3**

So what could she do? She called on the one resource at her disposal whom she knew could remedy the situation before anyone noticed and the host's reputation was damaged.

Remember in the Christmas story where it says that Mary pondered all these things in her heart. She knew who Jesus was before anyone else did. She knew what he could do before anyone else had seen. So she decided to expedite his use of his power – the power of God that Mary knew he possessed.

Application

> And Jesus said to her, "Woman, what does this have to do with me? My hour has not yet come."
>
> *John 2:4*

Now, when Mom asked her son to help, note his reaction. He said, "My time has not come." Exactly what that means we do not know. What we do know is that Jesus did not want to do what his mother asked.

"Aw, Mom, not now!"

But, again, remember that Mary was a Jewish mother. "No" was not in her vocabulary.

> *His mother said to the servants, "Do whatever he tells you."*
>
> *John 2:5*

Mary basically ignored Jesus' reply. Without any come back or any apparent hesitation, she tells the stewards, "Just do what he tells you."

We don't have any record of any other discussion. Maybe there was a bit more discussion. Perhaps Jesus knew better than to waste his breath.

Regardless, Jesus complied with his mother's request.

> *Now there were six stone water jars there for the Jewish rites of purification, each holding twenty or thirty gallons. Jesus said to the servants, "Fill the jars with water." And they filled them up to the brim. And he said to them, "Now draw some out and take it to the master of the feast." So they took it.*
>
> *John 2:6-8*

And when the resource was applied to the need, the results were abundant.

Results

> *When the master of the feast tasted the water now become wine, and did not know where it came from (though the servants who had drawn the water knew), the master of the feast called the bridegroom and said to him, "Everyone serves the good wine first, and when people have drunk freely, then the poor wine. But you have kept the good wine until now."*
>
> *John 2:1-10*

The guests were impressed – at least the sober ones. "Most people serve the cheap wine after everybody can't tell the difference. You saved the best for last."

Isn't that how like in the Kingdom is – the best is saved for last!

GIDEON

THE STORY OF GIDEON is one of my favorites. Perhaps because I see a lot of myself in the man Gideon.

Need

As we read, we see that the nation of Israel was being persecuted by the Midianites. This happened in the course of history on several occasions.

And when it did, the nation needed a hero. Or, in biblical terms of the time, a Judge.

The history of Israel, if plotted on a chart, would look like a rollercoaster. The cycle would begin in good times when the nation of Israel was experiencing prosperity. All was good, the people were faithful and God was blessing them.

Then, they would lose sight of the fact that the blessings were coming from God. They became self-confident and self-sufficient (or so they thought). They saw things in neighboring nations that appealed to them.

They followed Baal. Worshiped other gods. Practiced other religions. Forgot God.

So God would send a foreign nation to persecute them. The rollercoaster ride would take a steep, downward turn. Persecution, famine, drought, poverty. Such was the case circa 1000 B.C.

> *The people of Israel did what was evil in the sight of the Lord, and the Lord gave them into the hand of Midian seven years. And the hand of Midian overpowered Israel, and because of Midian the people of Israel made for themselves the dens that are in the mountains and the caves and the strongholds. For whenever the Israelites planted crops, the Midianites and the Amalekites and the people of the East would come up against them. They would encamp against them and devour the produce of the land, as far as Gaza, and leave no sustenance in Israel and no sheep or ox or donkey. For they would come up with their livestock and their tents; they would come like locusts in number – both they and their camels could not be counted – so that they laid waste the land as they came in. And Israel was brought very low because of Midian. And the people of Israel cried out for help to the Lord.*
>
> *When the people of Israel cried out to the Lord on account of the Midianites, the Lord sent a prophet to the*

people of Israel. And he said to them, "Thus says the Lord, the God of Israel: I led you up from Egypt and brought you out of the house of bondage. And I delivered you from the hand of the Egyptians and from the hand of all who oppressed you, and drove them out before you and gave you their land. And I said to you, 'I am the Lord your God; you shall not fear the gods of the Amorites in whose land you dwell.' But you have not obeyed my voice."

Judges 6:1-10

They cry out to God for deliverance. God sends a Judge – someone to lead them back into faithful obedience. Enter Gideon.

Resources

Now the angel of the Lord came and sat under the terebinth at Ophrah, which belonged to Joash the Abiezrite, while his son Gideon was beating out wheat in the winepress to hide it from the Midianites. And the angel of the Lord appeared to him and said to him, "The Lord is with you, O mighty man of valor." And Gideon said to him, "Please, sir, if the Lord is with us, why then has all this happened to us? And where are all his wonderful deeds that our fathers recounted to us, saying, 'Did not the Lord bring us up from Egypt?' But now the Lord has forsaken us and given us into the hand of Midian." And the Lord turned to him and said, "Go in this might of yours and save Israel from the hand of Midian; do not I send you?" And he said to him,

> "Please, Lord, how can I save Israel? Behold, my clan is the weakest in Manasseh, and I am the least in my father's house." And the Lord said to him, "But I will be with you, and you shall strike the Midianites as one man."
>
> *Judges 6:11-16*

Now Gideon was not necessarily the one we would choose to save Israel. He was not the bold champion like Samson or David. He was more the accountant who stayed in the background.

But when he was called into service, he accepted the challenge. With some reservations.

> *Then Gideon said to God, "If you will save Israel by my hand, as you have said, behold, I am laying a fleece of wool on the threshing floor. If there is dew on the fleece alone, and it is dry on all the ground, then I shall know that you will save Israel by my hand, as you have said." And it was so. When he rose early next morning and squeezed the fleece, he wrung enough dew from the fleece to fill a bowl with water. Then Gideon said to God, "Let not your anger burn against me; let me speak just once more. Please let me test just once more with the fleece. Please let it be dry on the fleece only, and on all the ground let there be dew." And God did so that night; and it was dry on the fleece only, and on all the ground there was dew.*
>
> *Judges 6:36-40*

He first assessed whether or not his call to duty was authentic. He put out his fleece (literally – this is where the expression comes from!).

Once convinced of God's call, he gathered the troops – again, literally.

> *Then Jerubbaal (that is, Gideon) and all the people who were with him rose early and encamped beside the spring of Harod. And the camp of Midian was north of them, by the hill of Moreh, in the valley.*
>
> *The Lord said to Gideon, "The people with you are too many for me to give the Midianites into their hand, lest Israel boast over me, saying, 'My own hand has saved me.' Now therefore proclaim in the ears of the people, saying, 'Whoever is fearful and trembling, let him return home and hurry away from Mount Gilead.'" Then 22,000 of the people returned, and 10,000 remained.*
>
> *Judges 7:1-3*

Gideon, like most of us, collected all the resources he could possibly muster. Thirty-two thousand, to be exact!

But that was too much in the resource department – at least according to God. Too many troops. Send home anyone who really doesn't want to be here.

Ten thousand left – still too many resources.

> *And the Lord said to Gideon, "The people are still too many. Take them down to the water, and I will test them*

for you there, and anyone of whom I say to you, 'This one shall go with you,' shall go with you, and anyone of whom I say to you, 'This one shall not go with you,' shall not go." So he brought the people down to the water. And the Lord said to Gideon, "Every one who laps the water with his tongue, as a dog laps, you shall set by himself. Likewise, every one who kneels down to drink." And the number of those who lapped, putting their hands to their mouths, was 300 men, but all the rest of the people knelt down to drink water. And the Lord said to Gideon, "With the 300 men who lapped I will save you and give the Midianites into your hand, and let all the others go every man to his home." So the people took provisions in their hands, and their trumpets. And he sent all the rest of Israel every man to his tent, but retained the 300 men. And the camp of Midian was below him in the valley.

Judges 7:4-8

It's interesting how and why God told Gideon to keep those whom he did. He tested them by taking them to the water to drink. Some got down on all fours and bent face down into the water and lapped it up like a dog. Those men he sent home.

Why? Try it yourself. Get down on all fours and put your face flat to the floor. Then ask someone to sneak up behind you. You won't see them. In fact, you won't know they are there until the shove you by your backside into the water!

But there were some who knelt on one knee, scooped water into their hand and brought it up to their mouth to drink – keeping their heads up and eyes open to any enemy who might be sneaking up on them!

Much to Gideon's dismay (but to God's delight) there were only 300 of these wise men.

Application

*B*ut Gideon took the resources God had given him and applied them to the need, nonetheless. And he did it in a most creative way.

> And he divided the 300 men into three companies and put trumpets into the hands of all of them and empty jars, with torches inside the jars. And he said to them, "Look at me, and do likewise. When I come to the outskirts of the camp, do as I do. When I blow the trumpet, I and all who are with me, then blow the trumpets also on every side of all the camp and shout, 'For the Lord and for Gideon.'"
>
> So Gideon and the hundred men who were with him came to the outskirts of the camp at the beginning of the middle watch, when they had just set the watch. And they blew the trumpets and smashed the jars that were in their hands. Then the three companies blew the trumpets and broke the jars. They held in their left hands the torches, and in their right hands the trumpets to blow. And they cried out, "A sword for the Lord and for Gideon!"

Judges 7:16-20

Of course, God limited the resources in order to show the Israelites that it was only by God's power that they were saved and not by the mere numbers of Israelites that were pressed into battle against Midian.

To understand Gideon's strategy, you must understand something of battle strategy in the Old Testament times. When armies went out to battle, the first line carried with them trumpets and, at night, lanterns consisting of torches inside of jars.

Behind the first line were the warriors. An enemy could judge the size of the invading army by the number of lanterns seen or the volume of trumpets they heard.

Gideon gave trumpets and lanterns to the entire number of soldiers at his disposal. He then arrayed them, encircling the Midianite camp.

So when the trumpets were blown and the torches revealed, the Midianites assumed there were thousands of warriors backing up the 300 they could see and hear.

They panicked!

Every man stood in his place around the camp, and all the army ran. They cried out and fled. When they blew the 300 trumpets, the Lord set every man's sword against his comrade and against all the army. And the army fled as far as Beth-shittah toward Zererah, as far as the border of Abel-meholah, by Tabbath.

Judges 7:21-22

Results

> And the men of Israel were called out from Naphtali and from Asher and from all Manasseh, and they pursued after Midian. Gideon sent messengers throughout all the hill country of Ephraim, saying, "Come down against the Midianites and capture the waters against them, as far as Beth-barah, and also the Jordan." So all the men of Ephraim were called out, and they captured the waters as far as Beth-barah, and also the Jordan. And they captured the two princes of Midian, Oreb and Zeeb. They killed Oreb at the rock of Oreb, and Zeeb they killed at the winepress of Zeeb. Then they pursued Midian, and they brought the heads of Oreb and Zeeb to Gideon across the Jordan.

Judges 7:23-25

The results, as expected, were abundant. History records that, after this tremendous upset, Gideon judged Israel in a time of peace that lasted 40 years!

Here, again, we see the repeating pattern revealed throughout the Bible. An apparent need is realized. The resources available to meet the need are assessed. The resources are applied to the need and the results are abundant.

THE CREATION OF WOMAN

I SHARE ONE LAST EXAMPLE of this repeating scriptural pattern. This passage is, perhaps, the best example of all. And it was revealed to me through a sixth-grade student during the contest I mentioned earlier. I was blown away by the insight of this young lady.

I shared my amazement with her parents, whom I believe are a big reason why she is able to see what I for years, and a whole congregation of experienced Christians over the course of several weeks, had overlooked.

And so I dedicate this section of the book to a young lady named Brenli.

Need

*I*n the process of creating the heavens and the earth, even God himself experienced a need. He had created the earth and the sky the waters in the land and all the plants of the earth.

He had put the man in the Garden of Eden to "work it and keep it." It was then that God saw a problem.

> *Then the Lord God said, "It is not good that the man should be alone; I will make him a helper fit for him."*
>
> **Genesis 2:18**

Soon after creating Adam, God took notice of his work and decided, "That boy needs help!" Guys, I am sorry, but we were not created to carry the load alone. As much as we think we can handle everything ourselves, it's just not in our nature to do all or be all. We need help (some of us more than others, of course).

Resources

*H*aving at his disposal all of creation, one was able to bring a plethora of resources to apply to the problem:

> *Now out of the ground the Lord God had formed every beast of the field and every bird of the heavens and brought them to the man to see what he would call them. And whatever the man called every living creature, that was its name. The man gave names to all livestock and to the birds of the heavens and to every beast of the field.*
>
> **Genesis 2:19-20a**

Interesting that God started with the most basic of resources – dirt. In the beginning, God created the heavens and the earth. The Earth consisted of air, water and...dirt.

It was from dirt that the rest of creation emerged. Plants sprouted and grew from the dirt. Adam himself was created from dirt. His name even bears the essence of dirt. So it was that, from dirt, God creates all other resources to meet the need at hand.

Application

*D*espite *the abundance of resources available, however, a* suitable helper for Adam was not found. The need had not been met. So God turn to Adam himself as a resource:

> So the Lord God caused a deep sleep to fall upon the man, and while he slept took one of his ribs and closed up its place with flesh. And the rib that the Lord God had taken from the man he made into a woman and brought her to the man. Then the man said,
>
> "This at last is bone of my bones and flesh of my flesh; she shall be called Woman, because she was taken out of Man."
>
> *Genesis 2:21-23*

So the need was met. Eve was the perfect help-mate for Adam.

Results

Now one can argue that the results were not so abundant. Immediately after the story of the creation of woman we read about the fall.

One could argue that the creation of woman led to the downfall of man. In fact when God discovered their sin, Adam tried to blame the woman -- and even God -- for <u>his</u> sin!

> *The man said, "The woman whom you gave to be with me, she gave me fruit of the tree, and I ate." (emphasis added)*
>
> **Genesis 3:12**

Of course, we must never lose sight of the fact that the man as well as the woman were, literally, "guilty as sin."

To see the true results of the creation of woman, we must look past the story of the fall and see how God's original intent for creation was fulfilled. Without the woman humanity could not possibly have fulfilled God's command to "fill the earth. "

And so the creation of woman came about as a result of man's need for a help mate. The need was addressed, but only in part, as God brought forth a plethora of resources in the form of all the animal species. But it was only in the creation of woman that humanity began to flourish in God's creation. The results were, indeed and ultimately, abundant.

One Final Example – the Story of the Bible

THIS REPEATING PATTERN can be found in any number of stories and books of the Bible. In your studies of the scriptures, look for this repeating pattern in the stories and passages you read.

Let me also caution you, however, not to superimpose this pattern over the scriptures. While it is frequent, is not in all passages of scripture. As you read, let the pattern reveal itself.

But now let me show how the pattern is revealed in the overall story of the Bible.

The entire story of the Bible reveals this repeating pattern.

Need

*T*he story of creation reveals at least three things about God. First, God needed to create – it was and is part of his nature. Second, God expects to be gloried in and by creation. Third, God desires to relate to his creation.

God created the heavens and the earth to be in relationship with them. But shortly after that creation humanity disrupted the relationship.

Being perfect, God could not fellowship with humanity who is imperfect. So a need for reconciliation is realized almost immediately in the story of God and his people.

Resources

*T*o this need, God applied an abundance of resources. The story of Noah tells us how God decided to start afresh with just one family. That family, as righteous as it was, failed to relate as God intended. As humanity again multiplied and filled the earth, sin crept in and dirtied the relationship it had with God.

God tried working with just one righteous man, Abraham. This relationship, too, was tainted by sin as the family grew.

God, through the great leader Moses, gave his Law to detail what was required to fulfill his will for the relationship. In hindsight, we know that the Law simply points to our sinful nature and sets us apart from God. No one, not one, is able to keep the Law perfectly as God intends.

God sent judges when Israel strayed. He gave them a king, against his better judgment. But even the great Kings David and Solomon were flawed with sin and the nation deteriorated to the point of division and exile.

God sent prophets as his spokesmen to preach, teach and even demonstrate in their own life situations what God expected, what he was seeing and what he would do if the relationship was not restored. All for naught.

But then...

Application

God knew what had to happen in order to restore the relationship. He knew humanity could not, would not ever be able to fulfill his requirements for relationship with him.

God requires punishment for sin. The only punishment adequate to make up for sin is death. For humanity to take that punishment would mean that God's original intent – to be in relationship will all of humanity – would go unfulfilled. All would have to die and be eternally separated from God.

So God sent his Son, Jesus, to live the only sinless life ever lived on earth. And, that life completed, allowed his only son to take our punishment – to die in our place.

The only resource that could affect the relationship between God and humanity was a "God-Man." A perfect example of what God intended in creation. A sinless human who would pay the price for sinful humanity.

Results

*T*he result of Jesus' life and death was punishment for sin. But God did even more.

He accepted the sacrifice as sufficient for sin. He then raised Jesus from the dead – resurrection. This was no resuscitation. This was new-life-to-die-no-more. This was, as Paul says, "The first fruits."

That is, God overcame death. Make no mistake, physical death is still part of the human experience. But it is not the final chapter.

With Christ's death, sin is punished. With his resurrection, death is not the end. It is the beginning.

Those who put their faith in Jesus as the one who takes our punishment and makes him Lord of life, seeking to live for him each day have much more than this earthly life to look forward to.

Death is simply the portal to eternal life. As we noted in the opening chapter, the new creation which ultimately awaits us is even better than the original.

We will be walking around the garden hand-in-hand with God. We will be eating food that needs no cultivation.

We will enjoy the beauty of the most wonderful part of God's creation. We call it "heaven." Jesus called it "Paradise." What better description of the abundant result of God's tactical work in creation!

Conclusion

MISSION. VISION. STRATEGY. TACTICS. Essential maxims in any successful organization. Perhaps to this point, people have not understood that these are biblical principles. God initiated them. God was the first to implement them. They are, therefore, tenets that we, as members of God's Kingdom, should adopt.

If we are to be faithful members of the Kingdom, we must seek to fulfill Shalom. All our activity must center on God's desire to reconstitute the wholeness that he created "in the beginning."

When Shalom is restored, we have a vision of what our world – God's Kingdom – will be. Unlike worldly, organizational vision statements, God's vision will be fulfilled. That is an iron-clad, written guarantee.

So, if we are to experience Shalom, we must choose to participate in the growth of the Kingdom. Our best efforts are required of God. Our success, though secondary to our willingness to give of ourselves sacrificially, is ensured by God.

We participate in Kingdom growth by seeking needs, assessing the resources God has provided to meet the needs, applying those resources to the need and then trusting God for abundant results.

Mission. Vision. Strategy. Tactics. God's design. Our instructions.

My prayer is that all who consider this "business plan" will find ways to make it happen. May God bless our faithfulness to his plan and his Kingdom!

About the Author

Dr. Marc Kirchoff is an ordained American Baptist (ABCUSA) minister. Currently serving on the staff of the American Baptist Churches of Indiana and Kentucky, he has 30 years of ministry experience. A 1979 graduate of Purdue University (B.A., Public Relations) and an alumnus of the Southern Baptist Theological Seminary (M.Div.. 1983; D. Min., 1989), his experience includes pastoral ministry in rural, urban and small city ministry settings. Since 1991, Dr. Kirchoff has focused his ministry in the area of stewardship. He has served organizations including Prison Fellowship, American Bible Society, and Crown Financial Ministries. Marc and his wife, Jill (Thorpe), have been married for 25 years. They and their children, Jonathan and Jessie, are active members of First Baptist Church of Terre Haute, Indiana, where Jill serves as Director of Children's Ministries.

About the Publisher

Leeway Artisans, Inc. was established in 2003 with the primary mission of providing Christian writers and artist the opportunity to publish works of literature, photography, and artwork of varying types. Our goal is to spread the gospel of Jesus Christ through creative products of inspirational value.

Leeway Artisans, Inc
9468 Pep Rally Lane
Waldorf, MD 20603